UPSIDE DOWN

BENNY PEREZ

THE CHURCH
AT SOUTH LAS VEGAS

702-361-1579
www.thechurchlv.com

Charisma
HOUSE
A STRANG COMPANY

Most STRANG COMMUNICATIONS/CHARISMA HOUSE/SILOAM products are available at special quantity discounts for bulk purchase for sales promotions, premiums, fund-raising and educational needs. For details, write Strang Communications/Charisma House/Siloam, 600 Rinehart Road, Lake Mary, Florida 32746, or telephone (407) 333-0600.

UPSIDE DOWN by Benny Perez
Published by Charisma House
A Strang Company
600 Rinehart Road
Lake Mary, Florida 32746
www.charismahouse.com

Unless otherwise noted, all Scripture quotations are from the Holy Bible, New International Version. Copyright © 1973, 1978, 1984, International Bible Society. Used by permission.

Scripture quotations marked AMP are from the Amplified Bible. Old Testament copyright © 1965, 1987 by the Zondervan Corporation. The Amplified New Testament copyright © 1954, 1958, 1987 by the Lockman Foundation. Used by permission.

Scripture quotations marked KJV are from the King James Version of the Bible.

Scripture quotations marked NAS are from the New American Standard Bible. Copyright © 1960, 1962, 1963, 1968, 1971, 1972, 1973, 1975, 1977 by the Lockman Foundation. Used by permission. (www.Lockman.org)

Scripture quotations marked NKJV are from the New King James Version of the Bible. Copyright © 1979, 1980, 1982 by Thomas Nelson, Inc., publishers. Used by permission.

Cover design by The Office of Bill Chiarvalle | www.officeofbc.com

Library of Congress Cataloging-in-Publication Data

Perez, Benny.
  Upside down / Benny Perez.
      p. cm.
  Includes bibliographical references.
    ISBN 1-59185-224-2 (pbk.)
  1. Church work with youth--Handbooks, manuals, etc. 2. Christian
education of young people--Handbooks, manuals, etc. I. Title.
    BV4447.P375 2003
    253--dc22

                                2003015935

04 05 06 07 08 — 9 8 7 6 5 4 3 2
Printed in the United States of America

I dedicate this book to my firstborn son,
Benjamin Jesse Perez II.

"A wise son makes a glad father."
—Proverbs 10:1, NKJV

You are the love and joy of my life. No young boy could make his father prouder than you. May the grace and mercy of God continue to shine upon you. May you prosper and be in health. May your days be filled with the intimacy of knowing Jesus. May your heart ever stay true to God's Word, and may your eyes stay focused on the prize. Turn your world UPSIDE DOWN!

Your mother and I love you with all our hearts, and we are blessed to call you our son!

Acknowledgments

My deepest appreciation to…

- My wife, Wendy. You have turned my world upside down! Your presence and grace have blessed me beyond words. Thank you for the hours of editing and all of your creative thoughts. Most of all, thank you for being my best friend, my most faithful supporter, my wife and the mother of the greatest son in the world. You make me look good.

- My parents, Jesse and Caroline Gutierrez. Your faithful support and encouragement have brought me to this place in my life. I will be forever grateful for the sacrifices you made so that I could turn the world upside down. I love you!

- Pastors Billy Farrar, Ken Squires, Jude Fouquier, Mike Robertson, Wendell Smith, Ken Wilde, Randy Valimont, Glen Berteau, Paul Goulet, Dave Stevens and Charles Gauldin. You have helped direct my ministry and have given me godly wisdom and advice.

- Julie Woge, Rob Howard, Trevor McCrea, Gerri Walrod, Rick Headley and all the Pacesetters International staff.

Your efforts have impacted the world! I thank you for your unwavering support of me and this ministry.

- My in-laws, Pastors Wendell and Gini Smith. You raised amazing children and have raised up a great church. Thank you for your support in helping touch a city.

- My friend Doug Shafer, who helped extensively in the writing of this book. Your talents and gifts are touching the world.

- My church and staff at The Church at South Las Vegas. Your passion to see a city changed and turned upside down is infectious.

- Iann Schonken, Jon Martinez, Doug Healy—my friends for years—and others who have stayed by me.

- Charisma House for having faith in me and my work.

- Most importantly, my Lord and Savior Jesus Christ, who has turned my life and world upside down. I love You and dedicate the rest of my life to seeing millions feel the wonderful love and acceptance that I have found in You. I live to hear the words, "Well done, thou good and faithful servant."

Contents

Section 3: Upside-Down Activity

Introduction

In the last major battle of the Revolutionary War, George Washington accepted the surrender of General Cornwallis at Yorktown. Proud, defiant and still in a state of disbelief at having been bested by the Yankee backwoodsman, Cornwallis ordered his smartly dressed British regulars to march out of the besieged town in formation. As they went, their fifer piped a popular tune called "The World Turned Upside Down," a powerful symbol of what the defeated army was feeling.

A World Turned Upside Down

That is not just an old song associated with a historical military defeat or a catchy phrase for dramatic emphasis; it is also a powerful picture of what happens to a person or a nation when it goes through an overwhelming event or faces an unrelenting change of circumstance.

Think of where you were that September morning in 2001 when the airplanes rammed into the World Trade Center. For several days, the nation was stunned as it reeled from the worst terrorist attack ever experienced on American soil. Do you recall the anger and sadness? Do you remember fallen heroes and brave rescuers? Can you forget the transformation of a president and the change in a nation's destiny? On September 11, 2001, our world was turned upside down.

But as powerful as that event was to rock our world and stir us to action, it is nothing compared to the power of the living gospel, which turned the world upside down two thousand years ago. Acts 17:1, 5–9 tells us that at Thessalonica, a believer named Jason and some of his friends were accused by an angry mob of turning the world upside down because of their continual preaching of Jesus. What an accusation…what an honor.

What About You?

God is looking for a generation that is ready to turn the world upside down with His power anointing. He is looking for people who are prepared to live and, if necessary, die for a cause that is greater than themselves. He is looking for young people who are preparing their hearts and purifying their minds so they can be instruments of righteousness in a world gone mad. He is looking for you.

Upside Down: A Guidebook for Global Impact is a tool that will help you to achieve the kind of powerful and persuasive Christian life that you have been hungry for. Hunger is the key. If you are not hungry for more of God, are not starving for a greater anointing or do not have an appetite to face darkness and see it brought down, then this manual is not for you.

But if you are ready to make a move that will revolutionize your life so that you can become an effective warrior that rocks your world upside down, then you are in for what may be one of the greatest experiences of your life. How can I say that? Because I am living proof that God can take an ordinary person and build into him extraordinary faith.

Introduction

This manual is a life story of sorts. You will see how God took me from an encounter on a Southern California beach and began turning my own world upside down—and it has never been the same since. Read how God taught me through His Word and called me into the ministry. Discover some of the powerful faith concepts that I have learned on this journey. Best of all, you will find out that the same miracle-working power that is at work in me is available to anyone willing to lay it all on the line for God.

But I have to leave you with words of caution: Don't plan on anything in this book becoming a reality in your life unless you are willing to pay the price of complete and total surrender to Christ. That is the beginning point for all of us.

Finding ourselves in Christ is where this manual begins, and in a way that is where it ends. Why? Because if we ever lose that identity, compromise that position or turn away from the source of life, then we will lose the connection, which is the source of all legitimate power on earth.

In Galatians Paul tells us not to grow tired in our pursuit of pleasing God because if we press in and continue, we will reap a powerful reward at the proper time. (See Galatians 6:9.) Are you ready to turn the world upside down? Then get ready to be turned upside down yourself because that is where it all starts. God bless you as you enter into a time of training, testing and perseverance.

SECTION ONE

Upside-Down Identity: Where Does It All Start?

Living a life that changes the world around us must begin with the life inside of us. We must become identified completely with the person of Jesus if we are going to transform this world and build God's kingdom. Just who are you anyway?

Chapter 1

My World Turned Upside Down

In the summer of 1986, I was walking along a beach in Southern California when I had a life-changing encounter with God. I had been backslidden for more than three years. At the time, I still attended church because my family went to services weekly, and it kept me from having to move out. Going to church on Sundays was a good trade-off for living at home virtually rent free.

My mom and dad were both strong Christians and wanted me to get involved in church once again. I knew both of them were praying for me to get back on fire for God. My mother often met me at the back door after I came home late at night. She would look at me and tell me that I was going to be a preacher someday. I would tell her I did not want to be a preacher, but rather an accountant because I wanted to make lots of money. Besides, why would I want to be a preacher and have everybody talking about me when they did not like the sermon I preached? I assured my mom that I was OK and that being a preacher was not in my future plans.

This story would play out many nights. My parents never

gave up on me but instead persevered in prayer for me. Then came my upside-down experience in July 1986. I was attending First Family Church in Whittier, California, because I felt my brother needed to get involved in a youth program.

The church's college group planned a beach camp at San Onofre State Beach, California. I remember that when the trip was announced, I was instantly excited to go. I thought it would be a great opportunity to hang out with the college girls in another setting that might be more appealing. So off I went to beach camp with motives other than meeting God.

When we got to the camp, I did not realize that we would have morning devotions and evening campfire services. For the first few days, I was not interested at all in the devotions or services. Most of the time I hung in the back trying to endure them so I could either go play on the beach or sleep in my tent. Little did I know that God was dealing with me and getting ready to turn my world upside down.

Turning Point

It started during a sunny Thursday morning after breakfast and morning devotions. I had tolerated the camp for a few days, and my heart was softening to the things of God. After devotions, the whole group went down to the beach to play and lie out in the sun. Toward the early afternoon, I decided to walk along the beach with my friend Paul. As we walked down the beach, we talked about our lives and relationship with God. Like me, Paul was away from God, and he attended the beach camp for the girls, not for God. However, his heart, like mine, was being changed little by little.

As he shared how he needed to get right with God, I echoed the same feelings. We both knew that we were not right with

God and that God was calling us back. At that moment, the Holy Spirit showed up on that beach and began to touch us. I felt the power of God come upon me. Instantly, I was on my knees along with my friend as we cried out to God for forgiveness. My world was being turned upside down in the middle of the afternoon on the beach. On my knees, I got right with God at a camp that I attended with the wrong motives.

After this experience, Paul and I went back to join the others on the beach to finish out the afternoon, agreeing not to say anything about what had happened. Later that night during a campfire service, the Holy Spirit began to move. A young man stood up and prophesied to Paul about what had happened to him earlier that day. The man then said that he would be going to Bible college. Shocked and perplexed, Paul looked my way to see if I had told anyone what had happened to us. I shook my head no.

I was elated that God was speaking supernaturally about Paul's future through a prophetic word, but the same young man then gave me a word from God. He prophesied that Paul was not going to Bible college alone, but I would be joining him. Everything came to a standstill as I heard the words come out of the young prophet's mouth. He told me exactly what I had prayed at the beach earlier in the day. The Lord had not only heard my prayers, but He answered them in a supernatural way. My life, my world and my destiny were turned upside down.

What Jesus did for me seventeen years ago He will do today for you. Jesus came into this world to turn it upside down despite:

- Facing opposition from men and Satan.
- Being accused falsely and charged illegally.

- Being ridiculed by his hometown and doubted by His own family.
- Betrayal by one of His closest disciples.

And yet He accomplished what He set out to do. Jesus turned the world upside down by turning people upside down. He is still turning people upside down through you and me.

In the Beginning

Man was never meant to be separated from God. We were created to worship God and be in fellowship with Him. But when Adam and Eve sinned through disobedience, the world that God had created was turned upside down in a negative way. Men and women turned from people in fellowship with God their Creator to people separated from Him through rebellion. Our world has been upside down ever since.

God wants the twenty-first century to be a century of the supernatural by turning our world upside down, but that doesn't happen in a church building. What do you want to turn upside down?

- Your school?
- Your family?
- Your city?

Then you need to see the power of God working through your life out in the "real world" so that a fallen world can right itself and get back in relationship with God the Father. If you are going to turn the world upside down, you have to be turned upside down yourself.

Half Empty or Half Full?

Think of it this way. Get a cup or glass and set it in front of you. You probably set it with the opening on the top. Why? Because the cup is designed to be filled with something, you would naturally turn it with the open side up.

What does this have to do with anything? Go back to the Garden of Eden. Adam and Eve were created to contain the power and presence of God. Just like a cup that holds water, Adam and Eve were created to hold the image of God in power and purpose.

But then the devil enticed Adam and Eve, and after a while they listened and agreed with him. If you let the devil talk to you long enough without rebuking him, you will end up listening to him. Adam and Eve were created with a divine purpose to:

- Walk in the holiness of God.
- Have relationship with their Creator.
- Have dominion over creation.

The devil came in and turned God's creation—which was good and filled with His glory—upside down. Sin turned God's plan and purposes upside down. Since then, the battle has been raging for control of the hearts and minds of men.

Back to our illustration. What would happen if you took that cup and turned it upside down? It would no longer serve as a container. That is exactly what happened to Adam and Eve. They could no longer be containers for God's glory and blessing.

As a result, the glory of God lifted, and the pair were suddenly "naked" in their eyes. They were not simply naked; when God's presence lifted, they were exposed. So God, in His mercy,

killed animals and made clothes for them, but these were temporary clothes at best.

God, though, still loved His creation. He had to come up with
a more permanent solution. In the Old Testament, powerful
men and women were used by God to bring people closer to that
original state of His presence and power. Men like Moses,
Joshua, Samuel, David and others were used by God to inch
toward the permanent solution in Jesus Christ.

But throughout the Old Testament, the people of God
found themselves in a cycle of being turned right side up
through the ministry of these great leaders, and then upside
down again through the opposition of Satan. They went
through a repeated pattern of rebellion and repentance.

Then John the Baptist arrived and became the forerunner of
the Messiah. John's message to Lucifer was this: "There is one
coming after me who is going to flip that cup right side up, and
you will NEVER be able to turn it over again."

- Jesus came born of a virgin.
- Jesus lived a sinless life.

The devil tried to tempt Him and get the cup to turn over
one more time. If Satan could only get Jesus to compromise,
the game would be over. But Jesus is our Champion, and He
did not fail like every other human who came before Him. He
fought through the temptation and won, and He kept that cup
right side up for all of us. Lucifer had run into a man who
could not be shaken. Satan knew he was finished unless he
could somehow destroy Him.

Jesus released the glory of God by teaching, healing and giving
people hope and forgiveness. Satan stirred up the religious
leaders of the Jews who were jealous and afraid of Jesus' power

and authority. Lucifer finally had Jesus brought up on false charges, which led to His cruel execution on the cross.

The devil believed he had destroyed Jesus, as all of hell celebrated for three days. But on the third day, the world was turned upside down when Jesus was resurrected.

- The power of Lucifer was broken.
- The power of death was shattered.

Afterwards, Jesus taught the people that the world, which had been hopeless for many years, had a renewed hope to be turned upside down. Jesus was the world turner, and He expects us to walk in that same anointing and purpose today. You do not have to live the way you have been living anymore. You can overcome the ruler of this world—Satan—because Jesus has turned His world upside down for us.

So how do we turn the world upside down for Jesus? It is not enough to simply declare, "I love Jesus." It is not enough to attend church or sing on the praise team. It is not enough to tell people about the power of God. You have to reach out and demonstrate it in people's lives. You have to invade their world and start turning their cups upside down.

Seven Keys to Turning Your World Upside Down

There are two sections of Scripture in the Book of Acts that demonstrate seven keys to turning your world upside down. Read Acts 17:5–9; 16:20–30, and you will find the following keys.

1. Serve King Jesus (Acts 17:7).

These guys totally surrendered their lives to the Lord. They submitted to God. If you want to turn your world upside down, you must lay down all of your agenda. These men turned the world upside down with their lives and teaching.

We cannot possibly turn the world upside down if we have not been turned upside down ourselves. It just will not happen. We have nothing to offer if our own container is not holding the presence and power of God. Simply put, until your world is rocked by Jesus, you cannot rock the world outside of you.

You must have a personal "flip" in your own life before you see the world flipping through your ministry.

2. Demonstrate a changed life (Acts 17:7).

If our friends and relatives and non-Christians are good at anything, it is recognizing a phony. If we are not acting on what we believe, then we will never demonstrate the kind of life that will turn the world upside down. True change means a repentant lifestyle.

The men in the Acts story were declaring things that were contrary to the law, which said that Caesar was the only God. If we are going to change lives, we have to demonstrate a changed life. This is what happened with the jailer in Acts 16. He saw Paul and Silas as men who were upside down, and he wanted to be turned upside down, too. The legitimate power of God operating in your life is attractive. People long to be set free, whether they know it or not.

3. Disturb the rulers of the city (Acts 17:8).

This does not mean go out and become a lawbreaker for Jesus. But there are times when you have to take a stand that will be offensive to some people. More importantly, there is spiritual wickedness assigned to your schools, neighborhoods and cities that you must be willing to stand up against.

Read Ephesians 6:10–18. Paul uses that letter, which was written to one of the most occultic cities in the ancient world, to show the Ephesian Christians how to deal with demonic strongholds. Some churches do not know how to deal with devils, and they are getting nowhere fast. They are not rocking the boat or getting rocked themselves, which means they are not turning anything upside down. We must learn to deal with spiritual wickedness.

4. Be willing to take persecution for the cause of Christ (Acts 16:23).

Persecution? Yes. If you are willing to disturb darkness, you must also be willing to deal with the consequences of taking a stand. Friends, family and foes will likely hurt you. Persecution is not just being thrown into an arena with some hungry lions. Persecution comes in many forms and shapes, including:

- Malicious gossip
- Being denied a promotion
- Not being elected to a position

The great news is Jesus said that in this world we would have tribulation, but we can be of good cheer because He has overcome the world. Jesus has already made it possible to turn the world upside down, and He faced the greatest persecution hell could unleash. You can take whatever the enemy dishes out because Jesus already endured it for you. You must be willing to deal with the consequences of taking a stand.

5. Worship God in good and bad times (Acts 16:25).

Paul and Silas were worshiping in prison. There was no reason that they should be worshiping the Lord, but they were doing just that while they were incarcerated.

- Instead of complaining, they called out to God.
- Instead of whining, they worshiped.
- Instead of becoming bitter, they were becoming better.

If you are going to turn the world upside down, you have to become an upside-down worshiper. Call yourself a pacesetter, a God chaser or a world changer—but unless you are worshiping God in good and bad times, you will never effectively turn your world upside down for God.

Why is worship so powerful? It is powerful because it causes a spiritual eruption to take place in the supernatural world, and it turns spiritual darkness on its head.

- Worship unleashes the power and presence of God.
- Worship increases our faith to do great exploits.
- Worship frustrates Lucifer because he was once a worshiper and knows its power.

Worship is more that raising our hands and listening to a worship CD. Worship must invade every area of our lives. It is how:

- We live our lives.
- We relate to others.
- We approach God.

6. Look for God in the timing (Acts 16:25).

At midnight, Paul and Silas began to worship the Lord. It was a new day dawning. If we are going to turn our world upside down, we have to believe that God's timing is always right. Do you believe that, or do you get frustrated when God does not show up on your schedule?

We must not only see God in the timing, but we must also expect the unexpected from the Lord. God does not only show up at unexpected times, but He also does unexpected things. If you are going to turn your world upside down, you must live in the unexpected. Why? The world thinks it has it all figured out, but when you demonstrate the power of God, you will rock their world, and like the jailer, the world will begin looking to you for answers. Live a life that anticipates unexpected timing and action by the Lord.

7. Take the God-ordained opportunities to share your faith (Acts 16:30).

Paul and Silas did not just enjoy their little songfest and say to the jailer, "Bless you!" They took the opportunity to tell the man how he could have his life turned upside down.

God will lead you into circumstances, and He will bring friends and strangers in your path. If you are going to turn the world upside down, you must be willing to give them the keys to having their lives changed. It is not an option—it is our commission. We must share the Good News with the world.

TURNING UPSIDE DOWN

1. What are the seven principles for turning your world upside down?

2. Which one do you need to work on?

3. Find someone who will keep you accountable to these seven principles.

4. Ask God for opportunities to share your faith.

5. Make a list of places that you want turned upside down (school, work, family or neighborhood).

Chapter 2

Who Are You?

I became the first Christian in my family when I was in the third grade. I was sent to a Christian school by my parents because they wanted me to get a good education. While in Bible class, my teacher, Mrs. Wolven, asked anyone who wanted to know about Jesus to stay in the classroom during recess, and she would tell them more about God. I stayed behind and gave my heart to Jesus. A dramatic change happened in my little life! I went home and told my mom everything that happened to me. I then began to pray for my family, and within just a few years, they all got saved.

However, I changed as the years went on. My heart grew cold, and the things of God began to fade away. By the time I was in high school, I had become a very religious person who knew it all but did not really know God. It took a fresh encounter with God to change the way I approached Him. I needed to get a firsthand revelation of God again.

In this chapter, I will show how knowing about God is not enough. Instead, we need to have a divine insight of who God is and who we are in Him. We need to understand *who He is* so we can know *who we are.*

Shortly before Jesus' triumphal entry into Jerusalem, which would end a week later with His crucifixion, Jesus had a conversation with His disciples. By now Peter, John, Andrew and the others knew Jesus and His teachings quite well, as they traveled together from village to village. On this occasion, as they entered the region called Caesarea Philippi, Jesus asked all of them this question: "Who do people say the Son of Man is?" (Matt. 16:13).

The disciples reported that some thought Jesus was John the Baptist raised from the dead; others thought that maybe He was Elijah or Jeremiah. Jesus looked intently at the men who had shared His meals and ministry for the past three and one-half years and said, "But what about you? Who do you say I am?" (v. 15). The disciples looked at each other uncomfortably, trying to grasp His question. But Simon Peter spoke up and answered, "You are the Christ, the Son of the living God" (v. 16).

Peter had a new revelation of who Christ really was and where Jesus came from. Peter was given a firsthand revelation of Jesus' identity. The Father had graciously revealed this to Peter, who was a simple fisherman. A new realm of understanding came upon Simon Peter, as if his entire life had been leading up to this crucial declaration. Jesus immediately announced that Peter was blessed for having been given this insight from the Father. No longer would he be Simon, "the unsteady." From now on, he would be known as Peter, "the rock." Peter had found himself.

Understanding Who We Are

Why would such an apparently simple conclusion be so paramount? Jesus had told the disciples all along that He was the

Son of God. What is so different about Peter's declaration? The difference was that Peter gained an understanding of his own identity because he understood by faith the identity of Jesus. To put it another way, until Peter understood who Jesus was, he could not begin to understand himself.

As Christians, we must come to the point that we know Jesus in order to understand our freedom in Him. Our identity—who we are—must be anchored in the reality of who He is:

- He is the Rock; therefore, we are unshakable.
- He is the Almighty; therefore, we are confident.
- He is holy; therefore, we are sanctified in Him.
- He is the Savior; therefore, we have eternal life.
- He is the Provider; therefore, we have provision.
- He is love; therefore, we have security.

Because Jesus is the great "I Am," we can identify with the power of His resurrection and truly understand who we are. I am talking about real, legitimate and unstoppable power to:

- Change
- Deliver
- Pray
- Heal
- Witness

Upside Down in Jesus

So what does it mean to identify with Jesus? It means that we know who we are based upon our relationship with Christ, and we believe everything that the Bible says can be accomplished in our lives as a result of that identification.

We cannot truly know ourselves without knowing our

Creator. Christians who are accomplishing great things for God have their identity securely in Jesus. They know God; therefore, they know God is at work in them. Remember Daniel's great words, "the people who know their God will display strength and take action" (Dan. 11:32, NAS).

During the time I was just getting back with the Lord, I was discipled in a class taught by a friend of mine who was a great man of God. I had been struggling with who I was and my self-esteem. My friend told me something that totally revolutionized my life. He said, "Benny, God's opinion of you makes man's opinion irrelevant—find out what God says about you!"

That statement was the phrase God used to catapult me out of a low level of living into the high living of the Spirit. I went on a personal journey to find out who I was in Jesus. If we are going to turn this world upside down, we must know who we are first.

God Wants You to Turn the World Upside Down for Him

During World War II, there was a famous recruiting poster that pictured Uncle Sam pointing at the reader with the words "I Want You!" emblazoned underneath. I believe God is saying the same thing to Christians all over the world: "I want you to…"

- Be a person willing to turn this world upside down.
- Stand up for what is right.
- Honor God with your life.
- Pay the price to see God's power touch a hurting generation.

God wants Christians to be His instrument to execute judgment on the powers of darkness in the world, just as Paul did at Ephesus when he battled spiritual darkness. He is looking for individuals, regardless of looks, race, social status and popularity, into whom He can pour His Spirit and power. Never turn down an opportunity to serve God, and never doubt your ability to do what He has called you to perform. God will work the miracles, but you need to know who you are in Christ in order for Him to do so.

It Is Not What You Know but Whom You Know

Knowledge opens many doors, but relationships get you invited inside. So it is with ministry. Greatness in ministry begins with relationship to God. Why? The closer you come to God, the more you will understand yourself and your limitations. Therefore, you will depend more upon God to accomplish His will through you.

If I go to the Microsoft Corporation headquarters and tell the receptionist on the executive floor I want to look around because I think Bill Gates is a great guy and a wonderful entrepreneur, I will have security on me before I can say, "Who wants to be a billionaire?"

However, if I am a friend of Bill Gates and I tell that same secretary that I know Bill Gates personally, I will be allowed greater access to the office. It is not what I know but whom I know that will make the difference of whether or not I gain access.

The Jews had seen Paul use the name of Jesus with great success. The difference was that they only knew about Jesus, but Paul knew Jesus personally. Paul had a relationship with Christ, which gave him the access and authority to cast out demons and perform miracles. In Acts 19:11–20 we find seven Jews, called the sons of Sceva, the chief priest of the Jews in Ephesus, who had grown up in a religious world. They were familiar with Jewish tradition and ritual. They were like kids who grow up in church but miss out on the real thing even when it is all around them. Just because their father was the chief priest did not make them better Jews, anymore than a couple's relationship with Christ will make their children Christians.

You Are Responsible for Your Firsthand Encounter With Jesus

The seven Jews unwittingly found themselves in trouble because they tried a firsthand encounter with darkness by using a secondhand light. In other words, their knowledge of Jesus was only hearsay—something they never personally experienced. In a court of law, certain testimonies by witnesses are inadmissible because they are only hearsay. These are words that the witness did not personally hear the defendant say; the defendant had supposedly said them to someone else who then relayed the information to the witness. It is ruled inadmissible because the witness never heard the defendant say these things firsthand.

The seven brothers tried to cast out a demon by hearsay—secondhand experience. What they needed in order to cast out the spirit was firsthand revelation, which gives supernatural:

- Ability
- Faith
- Confidence
- Wisdom

Without firsthand revelation, which comes from a personal relationship with God, we do not stand a chance. The demon world shudders at the thought of Jesus Christ and those who know Him, but they will always send a person packing who claims knowledge of Jesus without knowing Him relationally. Remember that it is not *what* you know but *whom* you know that really counts.

Relationship With God Is Built Through the Word and Prayer

When these vagabond Jews decided to invoke the name of Jesus, they got more than they bargained for. At some point we will have an encounter with darkness—the day is appointed. The question is, do you know Jesus? The seven sons of Sceva came across a demon-possessed man and used the name of Jesus in a secondhand manner. "In the name of Jesus, whom Paul preaches..." The demon's answer is interesting. He declares truth and tells the men, "Jesus I know, and I know about Paul, but who are you?"

The Greek text uses two different words for *know* in this passage. The demon says, "Jesus I know." In the Greek, the word *know* is *ginosko*, indicating "intimate knowledge and awareness of something by prior experience or recognition." The demon is, in effect, saying he is totally aware of who Jesus is because he knew Him before this occasion. This demon might have encountered Jesus personally. The demon remembered that Jesus destroyed all demonic power through the cross. Christ made an open show of them all, and at the name of Jesus, demon forces must bow.

The word used for *know* in the phrase "and I know about Paul" is in the Greek *epistamai*, which indicates "an understanding." The demon understood Paul's authority and therefore respected him, whether or not he had actually encountered Paul face-to-face. It is as if Paul's reputation preceded him in the spirit realm, and demons were aware that this guy was big trouble. Oh, how I want to have such a reputation in the corridors of hell! I want the enemy to know that I have an intimate relationship with Jesus and I know the authority I have in Christ. The world around us and the spirit realm are looking for pacesetters to take a stand and know who they are in Jesus.

These seven guys who tried to cast out the demon were asked about their identity. This is the trick and message of Satan to the world today. "Who are you?" is the question that he is posing to all Christians in an attempt to rattle their faith. As believers in Jesus, we need to continually affirm our position in Christ.

Recognize Who We Are by Realizing Who Christ Is

Jesus told us that the world would only grow more and more wicked, particularly during the last days. Our authority and position in Christ must be ever increasing if we are to be the pacesetters this world needs. Peter and James warned us in their epistles of our need to be armed and dangerous.

> Be sober, be vigilant; because your adversary the devil walks about like a roaring lion, seeking whom he may devour. Resist him, steadfast in the faith, knowing that the same sufferings are experienced by your brotherhood in the world.
>
> —1 PETER 5:8–9, NKJV

> Therefore submit to God. Resist the devil and he will flee from you. Draw near to God and He will draw near to you. Cleanse your hands, you sinners; and purify your hearts, you double-minded.
>
> —JAMES 4:7–8, NKJV

Notice that both Peter and James admonished believers to recognize that the enemy is very real, but he can be handled through a firsthand revelation and relationship with God.

Resisting the Devil Is Possible Through a Sincere Relationship With Jesus

The result of fighting a battle without the proper equipment was both humorous and tragic in the story of the sons of Sceva. The men were set upon by the demon-possessed man who ran them out of the house naked and bleeding, and undoubtedly out of the deliverance ministry. Like the old joke, they brought a knife to a gunfight and were beaten before the encounter even started because the demon had no respect for them.

I once saw a man at a golf course step out of his cart and approach the first tee. He looked immaculate, with an expensive set of clubs, sharp-looking clothes and confidence all over his face. He looked every inch the pro until he tried to play golf. He was simply not very good. He looked the part, but he should have stayed in the clubhouse where he was a convincing golfer instead of demonstrating his true abilities by attempting to play.

The Bible says that in the last days people will have a form of godliness but will deny its power. However, people want to be convinced. The world is looking for the real thing. People without hope want to see true power, just as Paul convinced the Ephesians of God's authority.

The World Is Dying to Be Convinced of Something Real

The results of Paul's ministry in Ephesus and the encounter with the demon-possessed man by the sons of Sceva were dramatic.

The Jews and Greeks suddenly recognized that the spiritual world was in a state of war, and they were seized with fear and began to revere the name of Jesus. Like the Jews who had been beaten, the Ephesians began to realize that there was indeed something special about the name of Jesus, and they wanted to know more about Him. Jesus was the only real protection they could have against demons, and they wanted that assurance.

I remember ministering at a local church in Apple Valley, California. I had just finished preaching a message on the power of the name of Jesus when I made an altar call, and a young lady came forward. I laid my hands on her and prayed that Jesus would touch her. Just then the young lady fell to the floor and began moving around like she was having convulsions. She proceeded to talk in a male voice and had unusual strength. The girl was demonized and had to be delivered.

I remember praying for her and the demon's saying to me, "I am not coming out, and you cannot make me." I was taken aback, and to be quite honest, I was scared. I stepped back with fear running through my body when suddenly the Holy Spirit filled me with faith. The Lord spoke to my heart and said that the demon was not defying me, but was defying God Himself. At that moment, I received a firsthand revelation that the demon could not defy God because Jesus had already defeated all demonic powers at the cross. The demon had to go because it was not my power but God's power flowing through me. With this added faith and firsthand revelation, I saw God bring a mighty deliverance to the young lady.

Catalyst for Revival

Someone once said that you know it is revival when the Christians begin repenting. So it was at Ephesus as believers began to openly confess their sins and repent before God. They wanted to make sure that there was no open door for the enemy to come back in, which meant getting rid of bitterness, filthy habits and demonic strongholds.

They brought all their occult artifacts, including magic scrolls, which they burned as a demonstration of their true change of heart. Many times I have had young people bring CDs, drugs, magazines, weapons and cigarettes to burn in a huge fire to illustrate to the world and the devil that deliverance had come to their lives.

These events occurred because the Word of God spread widely and the power of God intensified. The apostle Paul knew who he was in Christ and allowed God to use him in an extraordinary way. How about you? Are you receiving firsthand revelation from God, or are you trying to know Him from a distance? God's challenge to those who want to do great exploits for Him is to know Him, not know about Him. World changers of this generation know who they are because they know God.

TURNING UPSIDE DOWN

1. Do you have a firsthand revelation of God?

2. When did you encounter God for the first time?

3. Are you more like Paul or the sons of Sceva?

4. Take the time right now to ask God for a fresh revelation of Him.

Chapter 3

Cleaning House

Once the Lord begins His work on the inside, we have to allow Him greater and greater access to our lives as a whole. I believe if Jesus came to some congregations in America, they would not even recognize Him. Because He has not been invited in for so long, they would say, "Who are you?"

I want to show you four influences that must start moving in our churches if we are ever going to turn our world upside down. *Before the church can turn the world upside down, God must turn His church upside down.*

Let's look at a good example from the Gospels.

> Jesus entered the temple area and drove out all who were buying and selling there. He overturned the tables of the money changers and the benches of those selling doves. "It is written," he said to them, "'My house will be called a house of prayer,' but you are making it a 'den of robbers.'"
>
> The blind and the lame came to him at the temple, and he healed them. But when the chief priests and

the teachers of the law saw the wonderful things he did and the children shouting in the temple area, "Hosanna to the Son of David," they were indignant.

"Do you hear what these children are saying?" they asked him.

"Yes," replied Jesus, "have you never read, 'From the lips of children and infants you have ordained praise'?"

—MATTHEW 21:12–16

During His last week of ministry, Jesus came to Jerusalem and shook up the city. He did not stop and minister to the crowd but headed straight for the temple. Only a short time earlier, He had raised Lazarus from the dead in nearby Bethany, and now He entered the city a hero—but not to all, of course.

Jesus' Focus Was
Purpose-Driven and Intentional

In terms of a purpose-driven life, Jesus knew what awaited Him later that week. He would be crucified in a matter of days, but He stayed on track and remained focused. Some of you cannot even get your homework done at night. Jesus remained true to His mission until the very end.

What was His focus? His focus was His Father's house. Normally, He would take time with the crowds. This time, however, He moved past them and headed straight to the church. Why? God's eye is on His church. *Jesus had His focus on the temple in His day, and Jesus has His eye on His church today.*

Jesus Expects Purity

Take a look at how He drove out the ones who used the temple for personal gain. What was wrong with the vendors making a little money? The problem was that they cheated the people. They provided a service so people could sacrifice, but they made money on the side. Jesus had to clean out His Father's house.

Today Jesus is still cleaning out His house. How? Through the purity and power of His blood. We need to let Him clean out the tabernacle of our hearts. We need to let Him drive away any impurity. We need to respond to the conviction of the Holy Spirit, confess our sins and let Him cleanse us of all unrighteousness. (See 1 John 1:9.)

Why must we be pure and holy? We must be holy because the God we serve is holy. Psalm 22:3 says, "But You are holy" (NKJV). God is holy, and He wants His people to be holy, too. What does that mean?

God's nature, motives, thoughts, words and actions are pure. This means whatever God does—no matter what you or I or anyone else says or thinks—is right.

Everything God does is from a pure and holy motive.

God has no hidden motives. He is not like you and me who are weak and insecure and have to manufacture all sorts of excuses for why we do things. He is always pure in what He does or says.

Adam and Eve fell in the Garden of Eden because the devil attacked the character of God. They listened to the lies of the enemy who said that God really did not mean what He had said. Adam and Eve thought that maybe His motives were impure or His integrity was blemished, and we have been paying a price for their disobedience ever since.

Read this instruction from Paul:

> Nevertheless, God's solid foundation stands firm, sealed with this inscription: "The Lord knows those

who are his," and, "Everyone who confesses the name of the Lord must turn away from wickedness."

In a large house there are articles not only of gold and silver, but also of wood and clay; some are for noble purposes and some for ignoble. If a man cleanses himself from the latter, he will be an instrument for noble purposes, made holy, useful to the Master and prepared to do any good work.

Flee the evil desires of youth, and pursue righteousness, faith, love and peace, along with those who call on the Lord out of a pure heart.

—2 Timothy 2:19–22

We are called to be pure in:

- Life
- Motive
- Ministry
- Everything

Jesus Declared That His House Was a House of Prayer (Matt. 21:13)

Is your church a praying church? God wants His house to be a place where prayers are lifted up in faith and power. There is power in prayer. You are a nuclear time bomb for God, waiting to go off and explode with His glory in order to:

- Save the lost.
- Heal the sick.
- Encourage the downtrodden.

The fuse that ignites it is prayer. Your prayer closet is a launching pad for miracles. Prayer is the place of significance.

When I stand behind a pulpit, I stand before men, and that is awesome. I love preaching and watching people be blessed by God's Word. But in my prayer closet, I go to a place of significance because I stand before the living God, Jehovah-Jireh, Jehovah-Shalom, Jehovah-Shammah and Jehovah-Elyon. The Bible says, "The effectual fervent prayer of a righteous man availeth much" (James 5:16, KJV).

The Church Must Demonstrate Power

Acts 1:8 says, "You shall receive power" (NKJV)—meaning miraculous ability and power to overcome resistance. The church has been given power over:

- Sin
- Sickness
- The devil

In 1 Corinthians 2:4, Paul told the Corinthians that he did not come to them with mere words, but with demonstration of power. That is what we need today in the church. Paul said that the kingdom of God is not about words, but about power (1 Cor. 4:20).

In the Book of Acts, signs and wonders were part of daily life, were expected by the church and resulted in dramatic church growth. Signs and wonders were a catalyst for evangelism.

The Church Must Be Filled With People of Praise

The Bible says if we do not praise God, the rocks will cry out. Why praise? Praise puts God in His proper place. These four influences—purpose, prayer, power and praise—must become an everyday part of our lives and a part of the life of the churches we attend. The only way the world will be turned upside down is if they see something convincing for a change.

TURNING UPSIDE DOWN

1. If Jesus came into your temple today, what would He have to clean out?

2. Decide on an area in your life that you need to strive for more purity in—perhaps movie choices, unhealthy magazines and wrong friends.

3. Have you ever questioned God's motives in a situation in your life?

4. Take some time and ask for forgiveness if you have bitterness about that situation toward the Lord.

Chapter 4

Choosing Repentance and Restoration

There was once a young man named Michael in my youth group who got radically saved at the age of fourteen. Michael was on fire for God and was heavily involved in youth church. He was at every Wednesday night service and small group meeting and at church on Sundays. He loved God with all his heart, soul, mind and strength. He was an upside-down Christian, effectively reaching out to those around him.

However, as time went on, I saw Michael make some poor choices. He made excuses why he was not coming to youth church consistently. The friends that he had been influencing for good began to influence him in a negative way. Right before my eyes, I saw Michael's walk with God deteriorate. I often tried to talk with him and offer my help, but he chose to go another way.

When Michael backslid, my heart was crushed. How could this young man who had known and experienced God in such a powerful way turn his back on Jesus? I knew that the answer was not the result of a one-time whim, but a series of poor choices that he made. Michael relied on his wisdom and not the wisdom of God. He chose to run away from God's presence, not into His presence.

I saw Michael around town and prayed that the Holy Spirit would continue to speak to him and bring him back to his senses. Every time Michael saw me, he ran away and stayed as far away as possible. But I knew that God was working on him and that Michael was only one choice away from a life change.

Years passed, and Michael was nowhere to be found. I had lost contact, but God never did. One Sunday night Michael showed up at church again. He had grown older and was looking for a way back to the Lord. He kept coming to church until he finally made a choice to serve Jesus again with all his heart. Michael repented and sought restoration in his walk with God. This time Michael was not going to go back, but he was going forward, never to look back again.

Michael enrolled in our Master's Commission program and made strong decisions in his life to totally submit every area to Christ. His life took on a new direction because of his godly choices. He is now involved in ministry at one of the largest churches in his area. His life is a testimony to show young people that they can make things right even after making a wrong choice.

Choosing the Upside-Down Life

Do you know you have the most powerful weapon in the world at your disposal? Do you realize that you have something within your grasp that even God cannot overcome? It is called the freedom to choose. God gave you the ability to think and do whatever you like, and He will not interfere with your choices.

Now before you get too happy, remember that with freedom come responsibility and consequences. The Bible is clear that we will reap what we sow. Our choices become the most powerful weapons we have either for good or evil, for greatness or compromise. We will never turn the world upside down for Christ if we are not making the right choices in our personal lives.

The Truth of Consequences

You have the right to make the choice to hold on to God and all of the promises that His kingdom holds. In the Book of Joshua, we are told to "choose for yourselves this day whom you will serve" (Josh. 24:15).

The power has been given to you to make choices—good or bad. The decision is yours to make, but the consequences are not yours to choose. You have the right to make choices, but you do not have the right to choose what happens as a result of your choices.

Some people say, "I have the right to drink. I can handle it." That may be true. But you cannot choose the consequences when you get behind the wheel and drive like a fool. You do not choose the consequences that involve the killing of innocent people who happen to be on the road when you get out of control.

One of the greatest problems we have in this country is that too many people want too many choices. "I want my rights!" has become the battle cry of so many groups. It is great to live in a free society, but when we take advantage of our freedoms to make poor choices, there is a price to pay. The price of moral decline and compromise is sending our nation into a tailspin. If there was ever a time that our world needed turning upside down, it is today.

One of Them Lived to Turn
His World Upside Down

Let's take a look at two men and the choices they made. Both of them made bad choices, but one was able to make up the difference with a good choice later on.

The other was turned upside down by the world. Simon Peter's and Judas Iscariot's backgrounds were similar. Both were disciples of Jesus for the three and one-half years of His ministry. Both had witnessed the same miracles, healings and deliverance. Both had sat under the same teaching. Both men had experienced the same atmosphere of faith during the peak of Jesus' ministry, but now the end of Jesus' life was in sight, and the two had choices to make.

> Then one of the twelve, called Judas Iscariot, went to the chief priests and said, "What are you willing to give me if I deliver Him to you?" And they counted out to him thirty pieces of silver. So from that time he sought opportunity to betray Him.
>
> —MATTHEW 26:14–16, NKJV

> When evening had come, He sat down with the twelve. Now as they were eating, He said, "Assuredly, I say to you, one of you will betray Me."
>
> And they were exceedingly sorrowful, and each of them began to say to Him, "Lord, is it I?"
>
> He answered and said, "He who dipped his hand with Me in the dish will betray Me. The Son of Man indeed goes just as it is written of Him, but woe to that man by whom the Son of Man is betrayed! It would have been good for that man if he had not been born."
>
> Then Judas, who was betraying Him, answered and said, "Rabbi, is it I?"

He said to him, "You have said it."
—MATTHEW 26:20–25, NKJV

Judas Iscariot was called by Jesus just like the others. He served as the treasurer and handled all of the expenses for the ministry, but Judas had a problem. He had a personal ambition that ran counter to Christ.

The Bible tells us Judas made a deal to betray Jesus for thirty pieces of silver. He cut the deal, then waited for an opportunity to make good on it. He made a dangerous choice in his heart and then followed through, which was disastrous.

We Must Make a Choice

If we are going to be world changers, we need to keep in mind that everything begins and ends with the condition of our heart. We cannot turn a world upside down if our own hearts are impure. There are two important considerations when we make a choice in our heart:

1. Opportunity will either fulfill or foil the choice you make.

In the Old Testament, there was a man named Joseph who made a choice to be a man of commitment and integrity. He decided that he was going to live a pure life even if it cost him personally. The wife of his master tried to seduce him into a sexual relationship. She was after him day after day, increasing the pressure on this young man while her husband was away on business. But Joseph said, "I cannot do this thing that you want me to do and sin before my God" (Gen. 39:9).

Joseph paid a price for his integrity when he was accused of rape and thrown into prison. But God had other plans for Joseph, who rose out of prison to turn Egypt upside down.

2. You do not have full knowledge of what will happen when you make a choice.

Do you really believe that Adam and Eve would have listened to the serpent if they had known for certain what would happen after they disobeyed? Had they known that they would be separated from God's fellowship and kicked out of the Garden of Eden, would they have continued in their disobedience? We also are only one choice away from obedience or compromise.

Betrayed With a Kiss

As a group of men approached Jesus that fateful night in the garden where He had been praying, Judas stepped out from among them and, as was the custom of the day, kissed Jesus. This was also a prearranged signal, and the men with Judas arrested Jesus and took Him away. Read the story in Matthew 26:46–50.

How could Judas choose to betray the Lord so cheaply? How could he turn his back on the man who performed so many miracles? He saw everything that happened, and yet he betrayed Him for a few bucks. Why?

Judas never truly had a relationship with Jesus. He was in it for everything that he could get personally. He did not share in Jesus' vision of a coming kingdom; he was interested in building a kingdom of his own. This is the critical truth: Our motivations will affect our choices. How about you?

- Are your kisses for the Lord real or a signal for betrayal?

- Do we kiss Jesus on Wednesday night at church and betray Him on Friday night?

- Do we kiss Him when we are with our Christian friends and then betray Him to our non-Christian friends?

When Judas kissed Jesus, Jesus' words to Judas were, "Friend, why have you come?" (Matt. 26:50, NKJV). Jesus still loved Judas and called him friend even in the face of betrayal. I believe that there was still a possibility at this point for Judas to repent. Jesus was leaving the door of relationship open to Judas to back out of his decision, but he did not.

If we believe that God is only looking for a reason to punish us for our mistakes, then we are not listening to the God of our Lord Jesus. God is always reaching out to turn the world upside down. The world looks for ways to betray itself; God looks for ways to turn the world upside down so that it might be saved. If only the youth of this world would rise up and say to friends and enemies alike, "What can I do for you?"

What Are You in It For?

You came to Jesus because He gave you the most important gift you will ever receive: eternal life. With such a blessing comes a responsibility to choose rightly. You need to develop a mind and heart that says to the Lord, "You gave everything to me. What can I give back to you?"

Maybe right now you are at a point where you feel like you have disappointed God too many times, failed in your Christian walk or just made too many bad choices. But there is great news for you.

God Will Give You the Opportunity to Right the Wrong

Now, let's take a look at the second man who made a bad choice. This time, however, the Lord redeemed the decision. God gave Peter another chance to make right what he had made wrong.

Then Jesus said to them, "All of you will be made to stumble because of Me this night, for it is written: 'I will strike the Shepherd and the flock will be scattered.' But after I have been raised, I will go before you to Galilee." Peter answered and said to Him, "Even if all are made to stumble because of You, I will never be made to stumble." Jesus said to him, "Assuredly I say to you that this night, before the rooster crows, you will deny Me three times." Peter said to Him, "Even if I have to die with You, I will not deny You!" And so said all the disciples.

—MATTHEW 26:31–35, NKJV

Jesus predicted that Peter would deny Him three times. But Peter made the declaration that he would never deny Jesus, even if it cost him his life. How many of us have said, "I am never going to fall into this sin again!" only to find ourselves falling? Peter's heart was in the right place, but he was not prepared to back up his decision. Remember that opportunity will either fulfill or foil the choice you make.

How many of you have decided in your heart that you were going to become a witness to the Lord no matter what? How many of you are still waiting to witness? There will always be an opportunity to act on the choices we make—to make good on them or to back off.

People of Conviction Stand by the Choices They Make for the Lord

When given the opportunity to stand with Jesus during His trial, Peter thought about the decision he had declared. We find Peter waiting outside of the place where Jesus is being questioned.

Now Peter sat outside in the courtyard. And a servant girl came to him, saying, "You also were with Jesus of Galilee." But he denied it before them all, saying, "I do not know what you are saying." And when he had gone out to the gateway, another girl saw him and said to those who were there, "This fellow also was with Jesus of Nazareth." But again he denied with an oath, "I do not know the Man!" And a little later those who stood by came up and said to Peter, "Surely you also are one of them, for your speech betrays you." Then he began to curse and swear, saying, "I do not know the Man!" Immediately a rooster crowed. And Peter remembered the word of Jesus who had said to him, "Before the rooster crows, you will deny Me three times." So he went out and wept bitterly.

—MATTHEW 26:69–75, NKJV

Despite Peter's good intentions to remain true to the Lord, when the pressure was on, he failed the test. He made a choice and went with it. As a result he denied the Lord, just as Jesus had predicted. Let's take a look at the choices Peter and Judas made and the outcome of their decisions.

1. Both had an opportunity to back out of their decision.

God's grace will give us room to make right the wrong things we have done. If we do not take advantage of that grace period, then we have to face the consequences. Peter was given three opportunities to remain true to Jesus. Judas was given a moment to back off of his betrayal. They both lost their attitude of faith, and it cost them.

2. One man was restored, while the other was lost.

Our choices will dictate our destinies. Peter chose repentance and restoration. Judas was remorseful, but he committed suicide. Remember, *it is not always the first choice we make that is critical—it is the last one.* It is not about how you start—it is about how you finish. Peter started poorly but finished well because he chose the path of repentance and restoration.

Repentance vs. Remorse

God had a plan for Peter, but until he was restored through true repentance, there was no way that God's plan for him could unfold. Peter wept bitterly because he had a repentant heart. If you follow Peter's story through to the end, you will see that he was fully restored and became one of the great men of the early church.

If you are going to turn the world upside down, you will have to start by looking at your life and examining your heart to see what sin issues you need to deal with. You must take responsibility for your life and put yourself completely in the Lord's hands to be cleansed and set free from the addictions and choices that are holding you back.

Peter was repentant. Judas was full of remorse. One was restored, while the other was destroyed. What is the difference? The difference between repentance and remorse lies in the attitude of the heart.

- Repentance acknowledges the sin and involves a change in behavior.

- Remorse acknowledges the sin, but there is no real change.

Turning It Around

It is good to feel remorseful, but only if it leads to repentance. Maybe you are feeling down about a particular sin that you keep falling into. You are remorseful because you know that it is wrong, and yet your behavior is not lining up with your sadness. Maybe you have blown it so many times and figure, "What is the use?"

No one is going to love you as much as Jesus. No matter how low you have fallen or how many times you have given in to the same sin, Jesus is standing in front of you asking, "Friend, what can I do for you?"

Do not pass up the opportunity to get right with God who loves you so much. Confess your sin to Him right now. Begin to take a stand and ask God to change your behavior. Jesus will clean up your conscience and set you on a path of freedom.

There is no way that we can be world changers—people who are turning the world upside down—unless we are first turned upside down in our own lives. Are you ready to start turning? It begins with true repentance.

> If we confess our sins, He is faithful and just to forgive us our sins and to cleanse us from all unrighteousness.
> —1 John 1:9, NKJV

Heavenly Father,

I want to be clean and serve You the rest of my life. I want to turn the world upside down for You, but I realize there are some things in my life that have been betraying You in my witness for You. I confess that I have sinned in areas such as _____, and I ask You to forgive me. I repent of these sins, and through the power of the blood of Jesus Christ and the Holy Spirit inside me, I ask

You to help me make changes in my life that will be pleasing to You and will help me to become an overcomer and a world changer. In Jesus' name, amen.

If you prayed this prayer and meant it in your heart, you are free. You have also taken your first step in turning the world upside down for Jesus. Congratulations, and sleep well.

TURNING UPSIDE DOWN

1. What is the difference between repentance and remorse?

2. What is the result of true repentance?

3. Repentance and restoration go hand in hand. Describe how one affects the other.

4. Repentance is a lifestyle. When was the last time you repented, and how did you feel afterwards?

5. Choose to be a Peter and not a Judas.

Chapter 5

Going for Broke

Have you ever had your heart so broken that you felt it being crushed inside you? As a result, did you feel that rather than getting up in the morning, you would rather stay in bed? When I was younger, I had my heart broken because of a serious relationship with a young woman.

I believed I was going to marry this woman, and we had even talked about marriage. My heart was given completely to her, and the thought of us being together for the rest of our lives was a dream come true. We prayed together, did ministry together and dreamed together. I even thought I had heard from God that we were meant for each other.

All was fine until she had a change of heart and communicated to me that we were no longer meant for each other. The day she told me, I remember my heart sank. How could this be? I had heard from God; this was not supposed to happen. We had been together for so long, and now this had happened. My heart was broken, and my only solace was to seek God. I remember crying out to God and asking, "Why me, and why now?" Although I never got my answer, I did feel Him draw closer to me. The months of brokenness launched a new depth in my life that catapulted me into another dimension with God. I found God drawing closer to me and me to Him. Brokenness was my pathway to a deeper walk with God.

Broken Before God

When you first look at the word *broken* and think about what it means, it seems out of place. I mean, isn't the Lord all about fixing things? Of course He is. But have you ever heard someone say, "If it ain't broke, don't fix it"? God wants to fix—heal, redeem and restore—the broken areas of our lives. But FIRST we have to acknowledge that we are broken, and we must appeal to God through that broken heart.

Why? A heart that is not broken before the Lord is not a truly humble heart. A heart that is not broken says, "It ain't broke, so don't fix it!" We have to come to a point of being broken before God so that He can begin to shape us into the person He wants us to become. Take a look at this verse from the Psalms and see what value God places on a broken heart.

> The righteous cry out, and the LORD hears, and delivers them out of all their troubles. The LORD is near to those who have a broken heart, and saves such as have a contrite spirit. Many are the afflictions of the righteous, but the LORD delivers him out of them all.
> —PSALM 34:17–19, NKJV

The Attraction of a Broken Heart

Think about the last time you took out the trash. You take that container to the side of the driveway and hope that you beat the sanitation workers so that you are not stuck with all of last week's trash. Have you ever noticed the things your neighbors put out on their curb in the morning or the night before?

If you look really close (not too close), you might be shocked at some of the things people are throwing out: car parts, old bicycles, tables, sofas, televisions, skateboards and the list goes on and on. What is funny is that many times these items that are being thrown out are still in good condition. It is amazing what a low tolerance we have for things that are slightly old, worn out or out of date.

So we adopt the idea that it is cheaper to replace an item than to fix it. Sometimes that is true. But more often it is much more satisfying to dump the old stuff and have an excuse to go out and spend money on the newer version. We are a consumer society that uses and refuses. Unfortunately, this consumer mania has bled into other areas of society:

- If your marriage is getting "worn out," then dump it.
- If your debts are too high, default on them.
- If your church is not good, go to the next one.

But God has a use for broken things. He finds value in that which is broken. He uses broken…

- Soil to produce crops.
- Clouds to produce rain.
- Grain to make bread.
- Bread to give strength.

The Bible tells us that God is near to those who have broken hearts, and He saves those with a contrite spirit. A *contrite spirit* means "someone who is regretful or sad about having done something sinful." Why is God so interested in brokenness? How does this figure into living an upside-down life that will shake our world for Christ?

In Luke 7:36–50 we read the story about a little flask made of alabaster, a very delicate, translucent type of gypsum. It contained a very expensive perfume. Yet the woman who owned this flask recognized her need to give away this earthly treasure to gain what only Jesus could give to her. Read what happened when the little jar was broken.

Worried about his image and what people might say or think about him, Simon knew this woman was a sinner who belonged on the street with the rest of the trash. He wondered how Jesus could let such a woman touch Him and be next to Him.

The woman, in contrast, wept and humbled herself at the feet of Jesus. She knew she belonged on the curb with the other trash; she knew her reputation smelled like garbage. And yet, she knew what she desperately needed—and it wasn't new clothes, money or even a new reputation. She needed to get to Jesus and allow Him to begin to put her back together again. Notice what this woman did.

She Came Into the Room and Humbled Herself at the Feet of Jesus

She brought an expensive gift that she wanted to give Jesus. She took the expensive gift of perfume, anointed His feet with it and wiped His feet with her hair. The woman's tears streamed down her face, dripping on the weather-beaten feet of Jesus. Her brokenness and humble spirit actually ministered to God.

On the flip side, Simon, the religious man, sat unmoved by the demonstration of brokenness and humility. Instead, he was more concerned with how it looked and what kind of woman this was who came to Jesus. Simon's hard religious heart was more concerned about how things looked on the outside rather than the condition of the heart on the inside.

Immediately, Jesus addressed Simon's attitude, showing him that true brokenness understood its condition apart from God. People who have been forgiven much love much. This woman was broken because she knew what she deserved, yet Jesus offered forgiveness and mercy. This woman demonstrated that God is drawn to brokenness and the brokenhearted.

What Draws God to the Brokenhearted?

Broken people are not phony, and they are beyond playing games. They do not need a front or to pretend to be someone they are not. What you see is who they are. When you hit bottom, there is no other way to go except up. You are forced to look back to God versus your own wisdom. You cannot look to others because by now most people have abandoned you. You begin to earnestly cry out to the Lord, and He responds to your contrite and broken spirit.

Broken people also trust God. God is drawn to the brokenhearted because they place their trust in Him completely. They have nowhere else to turn. A broken person is completely reliant on God. In the psalm that we read at the beginning of this chapter, people who are broken are:

- Brokenhearted
- Contrite in spirit
- Afflicted

But God promises to deliver them all. Why? They cry out to Him out of their brokenness, and He responds. Do you see now that if you are going to become a powerful witness for the Lord, you must first come to the point and power of brokenness? I am not saying to get depressed. I am saying you must humble yourself so that you are broken before God—no personal agenda, no façade and no fronting. You need to be laid open before Him and be ready to be used by Him.

What Is Your Heart Condition?

Are you brokenhearted today, or are you looking your best and pretending to have it all together? God knows the true condition of our hearts. He wants us to lay it all down for Him. Only *then* can He take us and turn us upside down for *His* glory.

> I will exalt you, O Lord, for you lifted me out of the depths and did not let my enemies gloat over me. O Lord my God, I called to you for help and you healed me. O Lord, you brought me up from the grave; you spared me from going down into the pit. Sing to the Lord, you saints of his; praise his holy name. For his anger lasts only a moment, but his favor lasts a lifetime; weeping may remain for a night, but rejoicing comes in the morning.
>
> —Psalm 30:1–5

Will God come through for the brokenhearted? There is no doubt that He will. If you just read this psalm, then you can rest assured that God will come through. How can you be sure?

> Many are the afflictions of the righteous, but the Lord delivers them out of them all.
>
> —Psalm 34:19, nkjv

How many afflictions does He deliver them out of? He delivers them out of *all* of them.

TURNING UPSIDE DOWN

1. How does God respond to brokenness?

2. What does the Bible say about brokenness?

3. Have you ever experienced a time where you were completely broken?

4. What did the Lord work in you through that time of brokenness?

Chapter 6

Don't Tempt Me

Imagine that everything is going great for you: school, work, church, dating and so forth. And even better than that, the Lord has been blessing you personally so that you are lacking for nothing. Then one day someone or something comes along and threatens to take it all away. A robber is planning to steal it all and in the process injure everything and everyone around you. What would you do?

- Sit back and let him take everything.
- Compromise and give him a portion.
- Fight him with everything you have.

I think most of us would fight to preserve our world—especially if we knew that our families would be injured in the process. This chapter deals with the subject of temptation—one of the greatest robbers of Christians. We know that Satan is a robber—Jesus said so. But do you also know that we can throw everything away if we give in to temptation?

Many great men and women of God have fallen into

immorality because they allowed temptation to pile upon temptation. Many ministries have been wrecked and many families destroyed because a man or woman did not guard his or her heart.

What Is Temptation?

There are many definitions for temptation. Books have been written about it; movies have dealt with it. The dictionary defines *temptation* as "something that tries to persuade, induce or entice to something immorally or sensually pleasurable."

Temptation is not a sin.

A temptation is simply temptation. It is our response to the temptation that determines whether or not it becomes a sin.

Jesus was tempted but was without sin. If temptation was a sin, then Jesus, being tempted, would also have sinned. When you are being tempted, you have not crossed over into sin until you actually begin to give it your focus and start doing it. Some people will throw away everything just for a moment of immoral pleasure. Read the example of David, who did this very thing in 2 Samuel 11:1–11, 14–26.

Get this picture in your mind: David is finally the recognized king in Israel. After many years of civil war and wars against the nations around him, David is at a point where he can look back at some great accomplishments.

Instead of going out to war, as he was supposed to do, he was minding the business of the king. We need to remain fresh with God by always seeking new exploits for Him. David had gone from turning his world upside down to getting turned upside down himself.

David's Carnal Exploits

Lest we forget, God had used this man mightily. God is always looking to use a person who is available. David had grown from shepherd boy to king through a tough time of conflict, political intrigue and civil war. After a brief season of rest and organization of his kingdom, it was time for him to head out and do more exploits for God.

Instead of taking time for war, David chose a time of waiting, which cost him much. In the same way, if you miss your season, you are going to miss your moment. Some of you feel like your season is:

- Just being a student in high school or college.
- Just being an athlete or a musician.
- Enjoying life before you get serious.

But God says you are in a season right now where He wants you to do great exploits for Him—not next week, next year or even tomorrow—RIGHT NOW. This is your season to do something great for God. You are under authority to exercise greatness for God.

David's Lost Moment

David lost his purpose and vision. (See 2 Samuel 11:1.) David's purpose was to go to war. There was a definite season in a king's life to lead his army into battle. It was not his responsibility to tell others to do it. David's purpose should have led him to battle; instead, his decision to abdicate his role led him to the balcony.

David became lax in his leadership; he remained in Jerusalem. David's decision to relax during his season led to a relaxation of his morality. Likewise, when we are not doing the things God has called us to do, our natural tendency is to degrade into personal pleasure and selfish ambition. David lost his sense of direction and was now on a collision course with sin, which would change his kingdom forever. The same happens to us if we remain stationary when we should be running forward.

Have you ever noticed how much more effective you are in battling temptation or praying with somebody when you are in His will for a particular season? It is because God's anointing is on the present moment. If we step out from under the umbrella of obedience, we find ourselves susceptible to sin.

Think of the last time you were overcome by a sin issue. You gave in to that thing and probably regretted it later on. What was going on in your life at that point? Most likely you had gotten out of the game and thought you could coast for a while.

You Cannot Coast Through Your Season of Anointing

The Bible says we are to be watchful and vigilant because our enemy seeks to devour us. If he finds a blind spot or a weak point, he will take advantage of it. The only way to remain on our guard is to be active in our season.

David looked for other opportunities. (See 2 Samuel 11:2.) His wandering eye finally focused on something. Because he chose to stay home for the season, he became restless. He wandered to his balcony, and what do you know? There was temptation waiting to discover him.

I cannot stress enough that if you do not do what God is calling you to do, you will find something to do in its place. David allowed his mind and heart to stray. If he had only gone with his troops as the season called him to do. Instead, he tried to fill the void of inactivity with something else, and he found it.

God created us to be productive people. He wired us to respond to challenges and fulfill destinies. If we are not in pursuit of the things of God in the seasons that He calls us to do those things, we will fall to something else to fill that desire for accomplishment or activity.

If We Play With Temptation, We Will Fall Into It

David lusted as he looked. (See 2 Samuel 11:3–4.) The Bible tells us that God will always provide a way of escape when we are tempted. The problem is that we have to want to escape. I have heard of people who struggled with alcohol or pornography and thought that if they kept some of it around, it would help them overcome the temptation. That is like putting the mouse in charge of watching the cheese.

What is the point? David should have walked away from what he saw, but because he had lost his vision, he cast off restraint.

David had sex with Bathsheba. (See 2 Samuel 11:4.) He did what he knew was wrong. David followed through and did exactly what his mind and eyes focused on. It was not enough that he toyed with the idea—he let it toy with him. Pretty soon he found himself being taken away in his lust. He lost control and was dragged away. James puts it even better:

> Each one is tempted when, by his own evil desire, he is dragged away and enticed. Then, after desire has conceived, it gives birth to sin; and sin, when it is full-grown, gives birth to death.
>
> —JAMES 1:14–15

We Will Behave the Way We Think

The lesson here is that whatever we play with in our minds, we will eventually begin manifesting in our lives. If the Word of God is in our minds, then we can become people of power and purpose. But stop and think about what has been dumped into your mind lately:

- What movies have you been watching?
- What Internet sites have you been visiting?
- What kind of music are you listening to?
- What dating relationships are you getting yourself into?

None of these are in and of themselves evil, but when we abuse them, we can become ensnared and "dragged away" by our own lusts. There is a point that becomes a point of no return. We need to learn to get out of the way of temptation before we cross that line. We need to be like Joseph who was willing to go to prison rather than offend the Lord by sleeping with his master's wife.

David lacked any sense, as his crime led to a cover-up. (See 2 Samuel 11:6–25.) If there was one thing that David should have learned by now, it was that you cannot hide your sin from God. Instead of making it right, David attempted to cover up the sin. He first tried deceit. When that didn't work, he resorted to murder. Ever since Eden, men have tried to cover their shame and guilt, but God has provided the only way out of that situation—the work of Jesus Christ on the cross.

God Will Call Us to Account

There is no hiding from God. If you are in sin right now, you need to turn to God, ask Him to forgive you and then repent of that sin. There is no amount of hiding or glossing over that will do the trick. Only true repentance on your part will take away the guilt of your sin.

God sent a prophet to convict David of his sins. It is amazing how much God loves us. He cares enough about us that He will send people, circumstances and various attention-getters our way in order to drive us back into His arms. With David, he sent a prophet by the name of Nathan. Read of Nathan's encounter with David in 2 Samuel 12:1–13.

Faced with the prophet's accusation, David did two things that helped him begin to recover his relationship with the Lord—he acknowledged his sin, and he repented. Rather than harden his heart and run, David humbled himself and repented. David did what was required of him before the Lord. He confessed his sin. It is one of the most heartfelt confessions in the Bible. David confessed his sin before God and asked the Lord's forgiveness. In Psalm 51, he asked God to do these things:

- *Create a clean heart inside of him* (v. 10). David understood that if he was to relate to a holy God, he must do it from a posture of purity and cleansing. God cannot look upon sin without judging it.

- *Renew a right spirit within him* (v. 10). As David's heart became clean through confession, he realized that his rebellious spirit must also be tamed. Our spirits must conform to the Spirit of God.

- *Keep him in God's presence* (v. 11). The only place to go when we have sinned is toward God, not away from Him.

- *Allow the Holy Spirit to remain in him* (v. 11). The Bible says we are to be filled continually with the Holy Spirit.

Receiving the Holy Spirit is not just a one-time action. It is an ongoing relationship with the Father.

- *Restore the joy of God's salvation* (v. 12). The prophet Nehemiah wrote that "the joy of the Lord" shall be our strength. David knew that joy reflects a living and healthy relationship with God. Happiness comes and goes with circumstances; joy is an ever-present reality that is based upon our relationship with God.

- *Grant him a willing spirit* (v. 12). Humility—the bottom line to living a powerful life in the Lord—is living a life of humility. Is your spirit willing? The flesh is never willing, but the spirit should be dictating to the flesh and not the other way around.

  Like a city whose walls are broken down is a man who lacks self-control.

  —PROVERBS 25:28

How Is Your Spirit?

You may be wondering how to renew the Lord in your own life right now. Maybe you have already done the balcony thing, and you want to get back to the Lord. Maybe you have fallen into sin time and time again and feel like it is hopeless for you.

What should you do?

- *Repent for any sin.* Do not just ask God to forgive sin. Be specific. Ask Him to forgive you of specific sins that you are falling into right now. You have to mean it sincerely. You have to be serious about your willingness to turn it all around.

- *Ask God to consume you.* Place it all on the altar, and then ask God to come down and receive it. It does not matter what you bring to Him as long as you are sincere in what you are bringing.

Are you ready to be used by God? God is looking for young men and women who want to turn the world upside down, but before He can enlist your hands, He wants your heart. Give Him everything you have, then give Him all your dreams and hopes for the future. God will use you in amazing ways if you let Him.

TURNING UPSIDE DOWN

1. What is the Bible's definition of temptation?

2. Is temptation a sin?

3. How do we resist temptation?

4. We must keep our eyes and minds pure. What steps are you going to take to make sure that your eyes and mind remain pure?

Chapter 7

Getting Lit Up

What do you think of when you read the word *fire*? Maybe some of you see images of a warm fireplace during the Christmas holidays that warms your heart and adds something special to the season. Or maybe you think of a forest fire that is burning out of control and consuming thousands of acres of trees. Perhaps you think of an incident in which fire destroyed your property or injured a loved one. Each of these images are valid. That is because fire does all three of the above: it provides warmth to our souls, it consumes as it moves, and it can be dangerous.

The Holy Spirit and Fire

The Bible often connects the action and power of the Holy Spirit with fire. That is the sort of fire you and I need to light this world up. We need the fire of God. This fire will:

- Warm your spirit and give you greater faith.
- Give you boldness to see people healed and delivered.
- Become a destructive force to the powers of darkness.

Hebrews 12:29 says that our God "is a consuming fire." Matthew 3:11 says that Jesus came in order to baptize us "with the Holy Spirit and with fire." Why is this important? The answer is easy: the nature of God is fire. The Lord wants to consume us with His power and presence so we can become:

- Pastors on fire to preach His Word.
- Churches on fire to be places of hope and healing.
- People on fire to reach our friends and families for Christ.
- Ministries on fire to see people delivered.

The reason Jesus came was to set the captives free. At the beginning of His ministry, He went into the synagogue and read these words from the prophet Isaiah:

> The Spirit of the Lord is on me, because he has anointed me to preach good news to the poor. He has sent me to proclaim freedom for the prisoners and recovery of sight for the blind, to release the oppressed, to proclaim the year of the Lord's favor.
>
> —LUKE 4:18–19

Jesus' mission at that time was to:

- Preach the Good News (evangelism).
- Proclaim freedom for prisoners (encouraging others).
- Recover sight for the blind (healing).
- Release the oppressed (deliverance).

In short, Jesus' mission was to turn the world upside down, and we have that mission today. Jesus expects us to be people consumed with the fire and passion of the Holy Spirit so that we can also preach the Good News, encourage the hopeless, heal the sick and deliver the oppressed. This can only happen as we give ourselves over to the Holy Spirit and by being continually filled with Him.

We must first answer these questions: Who is the Holy Spirit? How do we become people consumed with the fire and Spirit of God? How can the Holy Spirit become real to us?

The Holy Spirit Is God

> Now the Lord is the Spirit; and where the Spirit of the Lord is, there is liberty.
> —2 Corinthians 3:17, NKJV

He is not a mist or cloud; He is not a mass of energy that comes from God. The Holy Spirit is a person. He is one of the Trinity that makes up the Father, Son and Holy Spirit. Like God, He knows all things, is everywhere and is eternal. (See 1 Corinthians 2:10–11; Psalm 139:7–10; Hebrews 9:14.)

The Holy Spirit Is a Person

> And grieve not the holy Spirit of God.
> —Ephesians 4:30, KJV

Again, the Holy Spirit is not a vapor. He is a real person with real feelings. He has personality and motive and is in complete agreement with the Father and Son. He can be grieved, or He can be made joyful. You cannot grieve a vapor. The Holy Spirit:

- Has a mind: "the mind of the Spirit" (Rom. 8:27).

- Has knowledge: "knows the thoughts of God" (1 Cor. 2:11).

- Possesses affection: "the love of the Spirit" (Rom. 15:30).

- Has a will: "distributing to each one individually as He wills" (1 Cor. 12:11, NKJV).

The Holy Spirit Has a Mission

The purpose of the Holy Spirit is to be involved in the work and plan of God, to bring glory to the Father through believers and to assist them in their spiritual journey. He has done this throughout the history of mankind and through the revelation of God's redemption of man. He has been at work and continues to work in these areas:

- *Creation.* God used the Spirit in the creation of the world. (See Genesis 1:2; Psalm 104:30.) The Spirit was present in the creation of the first man. (See Genesis 1:26–27.)

- *Revelation.* The prophets of old spoke as they were moved by the Spirit. (See 2 Peter 1:20–21.)

- *Confirmation.* The Spirit worked with Christ to confirm His work. (See Matthew 12:28; Luke 4:18–21.) Their message was confirmed through gifts given by the Spirit. (See Hebrews 2:3–4.)

- *Regeneration.* The Spirit does His work by convicting the world of sin, righteousness and judgment. (See John 16:8.)

- *Sanctification.* In obedience to the Word of God, we are sanctified by the Spirit. (See 2 Thessalonians 2:13.)

There is much more to the Holy Spirit than this, but at least it gives you a picture of who He is. Here is the real challenge: The Bible says we should be filled with the Holy Spirit continually so that His fire and direction remain alive in our hearts. (See Ephesians 5:18.)

How are we filled? The same way we were saved—through

faith. Ask Him into your life. Seek Him. But make sure you do a few things first:

- Prepare by repenting of any sin in your life.

- Invite Him into every area of your life.

- Believe that He will come in.

The Fire of God

We began this chapter with a very brief sketch of the Holy Spirit. He is the One who represents fire in the Bible and who wants to fire up your life with His power and passion. Just what does the fire of God do in your life?

The fire of God calls you.

You remember the story of Moses' call at the burning bush in Exodus 3:1–8. Moses left Egypt because he murdered a man and then spent forty years herding sheep in the wilderness. But the fire that God had deposited in him forty years before was still alive. God does not ever give up on us. If you have a dream or a passion that has passed you by, stoke that fire, and watch God breathe life into that thing once more.

Moses found this out in a big way when he encountered the power of God. He discovered several things about the fire of God.

The fire of God is personal.

Notice that the fire did not just consume; it called Moses by name. The fire recognized Moses from every other man on the planet. God knows us personally.

That same fire is calling YOU by name. *Insert your name in the call of Moses. Place your name in the great prayers in the Bible. Listen to the voice of God, and you will hear Him calling your name.*

The fire of God demands a holy life.

Moses was instructed to take his sandals off because he was standing on holy ground. God's foundational character trait is that He is holy. That means He is separate and above all that He has created. What happened to Moses when he took off his shoes? He became sensitive to the ground he was walking on. The little pebbles and debris began to be bothersome, and he naturally avoided them. As with us, when we begin to walk on holy ground, tendencies to compromise or be complacent are magnified. We can no longer walk the same way. The movie is no longer OK. That music disturbs our spirit. Our standards change. God wants us to be a people who are on fire for His holiness and who will be sensitive to the world and people around us.

How do we walk a holy life? Isn't that impossible? Apart from Christ we can never be holy, but His death on the cross made a way for God to see us as holy. Beyond that, God has made a way for us to practice holiness.

> How can a young man cleanse his way? By taking heed and keeping watch [on himself] according to Your word [conforming his life to it].
>
> —PSALM 119:9, AMP

> I have hidden your word in my heart that I might not sin against you.
>
> —PSALM 119:11

The fire of God called Moses to a higher calling. (See Exodus 3:8.) Moses went from shepherd to deliverer in one encounter with God. It does not take God long to begin moving us to a higher calling—all it takes is for us to be willing servants. Moses was a deliverer for his people.

What is God calling you to? It can start today. In order for you to walk in the calling God has placed in your life, you must first recognize God's supreme control. He cannot pour the fire of His higher calling into someone who is not totally sold out. God wants you to live in the freedom of your calling.

The fire of God consumes you.

From the time they came into their inheritance in Canaan, God's people struggled with how to live in it successfully. But God was faithful as always and began sending men of God into the nation to preach repentance and revival. One of these men was a prophet named Elijah.

The story in 1 Kings 18:30–39 is one of the most dramatic encounters between light and dark in the Bible. After bringing the people up on the mountain to witness the event, Elijah challenged the people with a deadly question: "How long will you falter between two opinions?" In other words, "When are you going to make up your mind?"

God's fire cannot fall on a place that is divided or double-minded. If we are going to walk in the power of God's fire, then we have to do it with one mind and purpose—to live a life holy and pleasing to God. It is just like Joshua's challenge to "choose for yourselves this day whom you will serve" (Josh. 24:15).

Whom are you serving? Let's take note of Elijah's progress and discover how the fire of God consumes us.

God Is a God of Fire

Fire is by nature a consumer. It consumes oxygen in order to burn purely; it needs fuel to maintain its existence. God is like a fire. He seeks out someone or something to consume—be it an altar or a person. What is the reason? God wants all of us, not just part of us.

Notice the progression as Elijah calls upon God:

- He took twelve stones representing the past (1 Kings 18:30–31). Elijah remembered and honored what God had done in the past. The old altar represented past victories and an assurance that God moved once and would move again. *We have to come to a point where we can have old altars in our past that show how God has worked in our lives.*

- He repaired and built the altar with the stones (vv. 30–31). The repair of the old altar was symbolic of the broken nation that Israel had become. There were past victories, but now they were a defeated people. By building a new place of worship from the old stones, Elijah showed the people that God is always faithful. *We need to take the time to rebuild some broken areas of our own lives before God's fire can consume them.*

- He laid a sacrifice on the altar (v. 33). Elijah did what the Law required of him. In doing so, he was approaching God in the appropriate way. Sacrifice represents a price that is paid. Jesus became the ultimate sacrifice for all of us. *God requires us to live a sacrificial life before Him.*

- He prayed in faith (v. 37). Notice how he prayed. He thanked the Lord for turning the hearts of the people back to Him even before it happened. That is faith—calling something that is *not* as if it *were*. (See Romans 4:17.) God respects that kind of faith.

God's Fire Consumes Our Faith

Elijah watched as the fire fell. (See 1 Kings 18:38.) Elijah did everything he was supposed to do and then got out of the way and let God be God. In this case, God was fire. The fire fell and consumed everything. The result was that the people declared that God was indeed almighty—just as Elijah had prayed. When we have done all we can before God moves, we need to stand back and let Him work without trying to help or hurry Him along. *When we allow the Lord to consume everything in our lives, people will begin to declare, "The Lord, He is God!"*

The Fire Commissions

Before Jesus ascended to heaven, He told His disciples to wait in Jerusalem until the Holy Spirit came upon them (Acts 1:4–8). There were one hundred twenty of them in that room. When the fire fell upon them in Acts 2:1–4, it consumed them. God wants to consume His people. He is waiting to consume you. But He has a reason for the fire—He is preparing us for the Great Commission.

Jesus Commissioned the Fire (Acts 1:4-8)

Jesus got the fire started. He told the people to wait in Jerusalem until the fire fell. He commissioned the fire—He authorized it—to fall upon the people at the proper time. He did this in two ways:

- He told the disciples that they would be baptized with the Holy Spirit.

- He told them that they would be witnesses throughout the world.

When the Holy Spirit comes upon us, we are commissioned to be witnesses. The word *witness* can also be translated as "martyrs." When the fire comes on us, we are to lay down our lives. The Holy Spirit does not come just so we can speak in tongues or prophesy. The Spirit falls on us in order to make us witnesses. Tongues, manifestations and power are results of the fire of God. They are tools for the greater purpose of the baptism in the Holy Spirit, which is laying down our lives and reaching the lost. *The fire commissions you with power to lay your life down for Jesus.*

The Fire Commissioned Pentecost (Acts 1:1-4)

- First came the wind. Remember, fire needs air to burn. The wind came as a "starter" for the fire that was to follow.

- Then came the fire, which came and rested on the one hundred twenty, flowing through each of them.

Fire needs two things to burn: oxygen and fuel. Like oxygen, we are the starters for the Spirit. The Holy Spirit is the fuel for our supernatural lives.

TURNING UPSIDE DOWN

1. Have you experienced the fire of God?

2. Have you been baptized in the Holy Spirit?

3. List some areas where you need to walk on holy ground.

4. You have been commissioned to reach out and touch your world, including your school and neighborhood.

5. Pray and ask God for more of His fire to touch your world.

SECTION TWO

Upside-Down Mentality

The battlefield is in the minds and hearts of men. You have probably heard that said before. And how true that is! Once we realize our identity in Christ, we must begin the work of transforming our minds to reflect that identity. How do we do that?

Chapter 8

It's All in the Mind

Two verses from Paul's letter to the Romans are some of the most powerful words in the Bible. They speak to the two issues that can make or break the power and passion of God in our lives. If we get them right, we become transformers who can turn the world upside down for Jesus. If we get them wrong, we will be ineffective and weak in our faith.

> Therefore, I urge you, brothers, in view of God's mercy, to offer your bodies as living sacrifices, holy and pleasing to God—this is your spiritual act of worship. Do not conform any longer to the pattern of this world, but be transformed by the renewing of your mind. Then you will be able to test and approve what God's will is—his good, pleasing and perfect will.
> —ROMANS 12:1–2

Young people today are faced with pressures from every angle. Our culture tells us sex is good, money is power and fame is the ultimate high. This sort of pressure causes us to conform or become like the mold of the world. But remember, the world is broken. It has been turned upside down.

God has called you not to be a conformer, but a transformer—

someone who will transform the world and shatter the kingdom of darkness.

God wants us to be more than meets the eye. He wants us to be more than what is merely seen by others. He wants to work deep down inside of us so that the world sees His glory all over us. Where does it all start?

Transformers vs. Conformers

Read the Romans passage again. There are certain things that must happen in our lives if we are going to become transformers and not conformers. Check out the steps of transformation that will turn you into a fired-up transforming machine for God.

Our bodies must be presented to God as a living sacrifice.

God requires us to present ourselves to Him as living sacrifices. That means to give ourselves over to Him completely. He does not want just the parts of you that you like, that you feel are attractive or that you have confidence in. He wants it all.

In the Old Testament, animals were sacrificed as a way of coming before the Lord and having the Jews' sins forgiven. The sacrifice was an act of offering—to bring something before the Lord in order to gain a favorable response from Him. When Jesus came, He took away the need for animal sacrifice and became our all-time sacrifice. Now we can come before the Lord's throne as living sacrifices.

Our bodies must be presented to God as holy.

The sacrifice cannot be just anything that we want to bring before God. It must be holy. Part of the reason the prophets spoke against God's people was that they were bringing unholy sacrifices before the Lord, which meant they tried to worship a holy God, but their hearts were impure.

Our God is holy. If we are going to approach Him, it must be done in holiness. Praise God that Jesus has made a way for us to boldly come to the throne of God!

Do Not Conform to Evil Desires

As obedient children, do not conform to the evil desires you had when you lived in ignorance.

—1 Peter 1:14

The admonition not to conform can be found throughout the Bible. What does it mean to conform to something? To conform means to become like something—almost like being pushed into a mold and taking on its shape. We are not to bend to the shape of the world; we are to be set apart for God's glory.

Think of when you used to play with modeling clay. You could take that lump of clay and push, pull and bend it in all sorts of shapes. It conformed to whatever put pressure on it. In the same way, the pressures of life can conform you through:

- Friends
- Entertainment
- Music
- Internet

Has someone at school offered to help you cheat on an exam? Has that attractive person you have been dating sought to take things a step further? When nobody is home, do you visit Web sites that are normally taboo in your household?

These situations are just a few ways that the world wants you to conform. And guess what? Conforming to the world is very easy. But when you resist the temptation to conform, you are being transformed through your faith. God has called you to be transformed so that you can in turn transform the world.

- You are victorious in Christ.
- You can do all things through Jesus.
- You do not have to conform to the world's ways.

Inner Change and Renewing Your Mind

You must be transformed through inner change. What does that mean? It means that you experience an inward change that results in a new outward behavior. This can only be done through the power of the Holy Spirit working in you. Remember what you read in the last chapter about the Holy Spirit's fire? The fire of God is what transforms you.

Have you ever seen a caterpillar's cocoon? It is a great example of how God takes our old life and transforms it into something powerful and graceful. The caterpillar spins itself into a cocoon. After a few weeks, it metamorphoses—transforms—into a completely new form—a butterfly.

God wants to take our sin and deceitful heart. He longs to take the hurts of our past. He desires to take our failures in order to transform us into new creatures. The Bible says that when we become Christians, we become new creatures, and old things have passed away (2 Cor. 5:17).

You must be transformed through the renewing of your mind. Why does your mind need to be renewed? The mind is the entryway for all knowledge—both holy and unholy. God created our minds to be able to have an understanding of who He is and to be able to relate to Him. When sin came into the world through Adam and Eve, our minds became corrupted. They no longer function according to the Designer's purpose.

God cannot use our impure minds to accomplish His will. Instead, He must renew them by putting something new in our minds so that they function differently. This is done through reading and studying God's Word.

Read Psalm 119, which is the longest chapter in the Bible. The entire psalm deals with a man's love affair with the Scriptures. One of the most powerful verses in the Bible is Psalm 119:11, which says, "I have hidden your word in my heart, that I might not sin against you."

- Do you want to overcome sin in your life? Start hiding God's Word in your heart.

- Do you want to be transformed? Begin reading the Bible daily.

- Do you want your mind renewed? Commit to reading and studying the Scriptures.

Do Not Be Pushed In, but Push Out

The world will always try to get you to conform. Do you remember when Jesus was tempted by Satan? He tried to get Jesus to conform to the world system. The great heroes of the Bible were people who overcame the world's temptation to conform.

- Noah built an ark in the face of a completely corrupt world.

- Joseph kept his integrity rather than give in to the seduction of his master's wife.

- Jesus went to the cross rather than having angels save His life.

It's All in the Mind

The world wants to cram you into its way of doing things and thinking. God does not want you to be pushed around. He wants you to be the one doing the pushing and to fight back with faith.

- When Satan pushes you around, push back by calling on Jesus.

- When your hormones are raging, push back by quoting scriptures that put the flesh under the Spirit's control.

- When your anger makes you want to lash out, push back by being silent and praying to God for help.

When you blow up a balloon, you are increasing pressure on the inside. If the pressure becomes too great, what happens? It explodes. Likewise, if we allow the pressure of the world to overtake us, we will explode and conform to its desires.

But we can call upon a greater pressure that is at work inside us. First John 4:4 says, "Greater is he that is in you, than he that is in the world" (KJV). All the pressure that the world can dish out is no match for the power working inside you through the Holy Spirit. You do not have to conform—you can be transformed.

TURNING UPSIDE DOWN

1. What is your thought life like?

2. Our thought life is a battleground. Jesus challenges us to go beyond the Ten Commandments. Have you conformed in your thoughts concerning a person, situation or even yourself?

3. Write down those thoughts, and look at them for what they are: destructive, angry and wrong.

4. Decide right now to target those thoughts. When they come flooding back, cast them down. Do not allow them to pressure you; push back and call on Jesus.

Chapter 9

Part 1: Winning the Giant Battle

We just learned that everything we experience for good or bad begins in the mind. We also discovered that God calls us to victory in Christ. It is time to rise up and take a stand for righteousness and begin turning our world upside down for Jesus. God is not satisfied with status-quo churches that do little from Sunday to Sunday except gather together, sing a few songs and pat each other on the back.

God longs to pour His Spirit into a radical people who will manifest His supernatural power and execute vengeance upon the powers of darkness. He desires a church that is an example of holiness and purity. He seeks a generation of believers who are not afraid to stand up and be counted among those who believe in and call upon the Lord Jesus Christ. God looks for world changers whose faith can turn their schools, churches and world upside down for Christ.

The Bible is full of upside-down believers who laid it all on the line in order to follow God's will for their lives.

- Noah was called upon to build an enormous boat because of a rainy forecast, even though it had never rained before that time.

- Abraham left the security of his country and family to embark on an unknown destiny in a far-off place called Canaan.

- Moses gave up the splendors of Egypt to lead an unruly nation to the Promised Land.

- Esther risked her life by approaching the king on behalf of her people.

I want to look again at the life of a man who turned his world upside down and forever changed the course of human history: David, one of the most revered and recognized biblical characters apart from Jesus. We love David because of his sincere faith, heroic encounter with Goliath, deep love for God, godliness and human flaws. All of these made David a desirable person to emulate and a perfect example of someone used by God because he was available and willing.

The story of David begins in the Book of 1 Samuel during one of the many wars Israel waged against their antagonistic neighbors to the south, the Philistines. As we look upon the battle lines that were drawn on either side of the valley of Elah, we see two different attitudes prevailing within the camps.

> Now the Philistines gathered their armies together to battle, and were gathered at Sochoh, which belongs to Judah; they encamped between Sochoh and Azekah, in Ephes Dammin. And Saul and the men of Israel were gathered together, and they encamped in the

Valley of Elah, and drew up in battle array against the Philistines. The Philistines stood on a mountain on one side, and Israel stood on a mountain on the other side, with a valley between them.

—1 Samuel 17:1–3, nkjv

The Armies Faced Each Other on Opposite Sides

There was a distinction between the two armies. There was no question as to which army a person served because of the distance between the two sides. Today, the forces of darkness are gathered to wage war against us. There were two distinct sides in David's time; there are also two separate camps in our own day.

We cannot be in both armies. We are either serving in the army of God or the army of Satan. God wants us to be either hot (running with fervency) or cold (completely self-absorbed) because being lukewarm is completely unacceptable. (See Revelation 3:16.)

In Exodus, Moses realized that without God's presence, all was hopeless. Moses presented himself and the people to the Lord and asked for God's special favor upon them.

And He said, "My Presence will go with you, and I will give you rest." Then he said to Him, "If Your Presence does not go with us, do not bring us up from here."

—Exodus 33:14–15, nkjv

In his wisdom, Moses asked, "Lord, don't even bother to send us out unless You are going ahead." Praise God we can expect that not only will He send us out, but also that His Spirit will attend us every step of the way.

The Armies Had a Valley Between Them

A valley in the Bible often represents more than simply an indention in the geography between two high points. Sometimes a valley represents a spiritual challenge. It also represents a place of uncertainty, such as "the valley of the shadow of death" in Psalm 23, a place of darkness and mystery through which God promises to accompany us.

The prophet Joel spoke of a valley of decision wherein multitudes of people were called upon to decide one way or the other as to whom they will serve: "Multitudes, multitudes in the valley of decision! For the day of the LORD is near in the valley of decision" (Joel 3:14).

The valley represented a combination of these to the two opposing armies in 1 Samuel 17. For Israel, the valley symbolized an uneasy buffer between themselves and the enemy. It was a place where they could not get hurt, but where they could not do much damage to the enemy either. Sometimes Christians come to a point in their lives where they prefer a valley between themselves and the enemy rather than risk a position on the front lines.

The Enemy Occupied Ground That Belonged to God's People

The Philistine army held ground that did not belong to them; it belonged to Judah. The enemy has made unwarranted intrusions into our lives because we have allowed him access. We must fight with the understanding that we war to retake what God has already given to us, so we can fight with greater intensity.

Fear's Façade

Fearful opposition always gets a response. Even the most faith-filled Christian can be rattled if only for a moment. The demonic world is good at instilling fear, and it thrives on it. Fear is one of the most potent weapons in the enemy's arsenal. If the enemy can keep a person off balance because of fear and intimidation, he has immobilized him.

When President Franklin Roosevelt took office in 1933, the country was in a deep depression, both economically and psychologically. FDR knew that he had to get the people to focus on the possibilities rather than dwell on the current realities.

During his inaugural speech, as he described the challenges that America faced, he uttered these famous words: "The only thing we have to fear is fear itself." He said everything else was possible to deal with, but fear would only lead to further panic and greater erosion of society. FDR was an invalid who could not walk as a result of infantile paralysis, which he succumbed to at age thirty-nine. Yet the man in a wheelchair led the nation. If anyone knew about fear and challenges, it was Roosevelt. He once remarked, "If you have spent two years in bed trying to wiggle your big toe, everything else seems easy."[1]

From outright terror by demonic visitations to more subtle fears such as the fear of failure, witnessing and taking risks, fear comes in many forms. It came in the form of a giant who opposed the Israelites in 1 Samuel 17: 4–7. Merely by his size, Goliath struck fear in the hearts of the people of Judah. His features included:

- Being 9 feet 9 inches tall
- Weighing between 500 and 600 pounds
- An armor that weighed 125 pounds

- A 10-pound helmet
- Leg greaves that weighed 20 pounds
- Breastplate that weighed 20 pounds
- A 15-pound spearhead
- A sword that weighed 10 pounds
- Shields that weighed 30 pounds
- A total outerwear weight of 230 pounds

The giant's name, *Goliath*, means "soothsayer," or someone who tells the future. This is exactly what fear tries to do to us. It attempts to dictate our future by telling us how things are in the present. Fear typically says things like: "You can't do that." "You've tried that before." "She isn't going to listen to you." Fear tries to foul up our future by paralyzing our present. Goliath used this same tactic with the army of Saul.

> Then he stood and cried out to the armies of Israel, and said to them, "Why have you come out to line up for battle? Am I not a Philistine, and you the servants of Saul? Choose a man for yourselves, and let him come down to me. If he is able to fight with me and kill me, then we will be your servants. But if I prevail against him and kill him, then you shall be our servants and serve us." And the Philistine said, "I defy the armies of Israel this day; give me a man, that we may fight together." When Saul and all Israel heard these words of the Philistine, they were dismayed and greatly afraid. Now David was the son of that Ephrathite of Bethlehem Judah, whose name was Jesse, and who had eight sons. And the man was old, advanced in years, in the days of Saul.
>
> —1 Samuel 17:8–12, nkjv

Part 1: Winning the Giant Battle

Who would not be afraid? No one in his natural mind would consider going head to head with this giant. However, a challenge was issued, and a response was required. Someone had to go down and battle the giant. This person not only had to fight Goliath, but also to kill him. Those were his terms. There are principles in that challenge that cannot be overlooked.

God's People Dressed for Battle, but Nobody Fought

Goliath basically asked Saul's army their intentions—whether to fight or not. Many Christians look good in the ranks: arms lifted in worship, Bibles open during sermons and always at church on Sundays. But if you put some of them on the battleline, their real spiritual confidence bleeds through. It is good to put on our spiritual armor, including the helmet of salvation and the shield of faith. But if we are unwilling to do battle when the day of battle comes, we will be as useful as a flat tire. In the Old Testament, King Ahab answered a challenge from the king of Syria this way: "Let not him who girds [puts] on his armor boast like him who takes it off" (1 Kings 20:11, NAS). Until our spiritual armor is tested in battle, we have proven nothing.

Winner Takes All in a Contest

Notice the challenge in 1 Samuel 17:9: If you fight and win, you will conquer us. If we fight and defeat you, we will conquer you. There are no other considerations. This is an all-or-nothing contest between God's people and the kingdom of darkness. It is a fight to the death that has been won by the death and resurrection of our Lord.

By dying on the cross for our sins, Jesus conquered death for us and destroyed the power of the devil to rule our lives. Jesus gave us the authority of His Word and the power of the Holy Spirit to defeat the works of the enemy in our lives and in the lives of others. How did He secure this? He secured it by obedience. Because Jesus was obedient, even to the point of an agonizing death on the cross, we have victory. (See Philippians 2:8.)

> For as by one man's [Adam's] disobedience many were made sinners, so also by one Man's [Jesus'] obedience many will be made righteous.
>
> —ROMANS 5:19, NKJV

Fearful Leadership Affects Everyone

Instead of standing up to Goliath, King Saul hid in his tent. As a result, he infected everyone in the camp with fear. If we are to turn the world upside down, we have to be the ones who will stand up and take on the challenge. Someone must answer the boastful challenges of the enemy. If the current leaders will not take up God's cause, He will find someone else with the faith to fight.

Fear Can Never Really Harm You

Despite all of Goliath's shouts, threats and marches before Judah, not one person was actually harmed physically. Fear can only hurt you if you allow it to enter into your heart and mind. The only real weapon used by the giant was words.

The Power of Spoken Words

Words can move a nation to action, cause a situation to reverse itself, increase faith and give confidence. They can also tear down, discourage and paralyze. As Christians we recognize that our words, when backed up by the truth of Scripture and faith, are the most powerful weapon we possess.

> For the weapons of our warfare are not carnal but mighty in God for pulling down strongholds, casting down arguments and every high thing that exalts itself against the knowledge of God, bringing every thought into captivity to the obedience of Christ.
>
> —2 CORINTHIANS 10:4–5, NKJV

How do we destroy the enemy's strongholds? We destroy them through the spiritual weapons we possess, our words engaging our faith. Paul says the effective combination of the Holy Spirit and our faith produces "spiritual thoughts with spiritual words" (1 Cor. 2:13, NAS). We might be able to speak with the eloquence of Cicero, but unless the words are anchored in the truth of God, they are fleshly and useless. We need boldness and courage to declare God's Word when the enemy tries to shrink our faith.

Giant Threats

The faith of God's people shrunk when they heard and listened to Goliath, who appeared even more imposing with his threatening words. The Bible says that everyone was dismayed, which in the Hebrew translates into the idea of a complete breakdown in attitude and spirit because of fear and confusion. Dismayed also means to be discouraged and terrified.

Goliath certainly scored points in the intimidation department. For forty days he railed against the army of Saul, holding them in a state of immobility because they were afraid of the things he said. The devil's ability and power to disrupt our lives increases if he can get us to listen and believe him. It started in Eden, and he has been doing it ever since. Jesus said of Satan:

> He was a murderer from the beginning, and does not stand in the truth, because there is no truth in him. When he speaks a lie, he speaks from his own resources, for he is a liar and the father of it.
>
> —JOHN 8:44, NKJV

The enemy is a liar, which is his nature. He sometimes mixes elements of truth with his suggestions, masquerading it as truth. We should not be taken by surprise when he comes to us with all manner of bad news. He is an expert in confusion, discouragement and fear. Many good people have fallen victim to his devices. In fact, the enemy even took me out to lunch one day.

Expose the Lies of the Enemy

I had just arrived in Marysville, Washington, where I had taken the youth pastor position. There was a young man who went to lunch with me at a local sandwich shop. After some small talk, this man gave me the bad news. He looked at me and with a smirk on his face said, "Pastor Benny, you're a nice guy and all, but I am telling you that you will not make a difference up here."

I sat there in utter shock, wondering if I was really hearing what I thought I was hearing. This man said there were too many drugs and too much partying going on for me to think I was going to bring about a change. His words hit deep within my spirit as I grasped the intent of the enemy. The devil wanted to paralyze me with the words of this man. I sat and thought for a moment, and then I told him, "You're absolutely right. I cannot make a difference, but Jesus will." Praise God! The lies of the enemy tried to rob me, but it inspired me instead to cling to the truth of God's Word. Needless to say, God proved that man wrong as we saw the youth church grow to more than eight hundred students, with hundreds radically changed by the power of God.

We are to expose the lies of the enemy and shed light on his intruding darkness. We must speak the truth in love and set the record straight that Jesus is the way, the truth and the life. The only way we can speak the truth is to know the truth—by reading God's Word and making it a part of our lives.

TURNING UPSIDE DOWN

1. Is there a Goliath in your life? Such as a fear that overwhelms you?

2. Can you recognize the lie in your fear?

Chapter 10

Part 2: Winning the Giant Battle

We just learned that the enemy is great at causing distraction and discouragement. If Satan can keep Christians off balance by instilling fear and causing strife among us, he knows he is in control of the situation, and it is the Christians who are turned upside down. So he presents a challenge, a trying circumstance or a giant in order to threaten us.

Thankfully, Jesus is never surprised by anything. When the enemy brings up a challenger, you can be sure that God will raise up a defender—a transformer—who will rise to the challenge and turn the world upside down for Christ. Biblical examples include:

- Moses vs. Pharaoh
- Joshua vs. the Canaanite kings
- David vs. Goliath
- Esther vs. Haman

God will raise up anyone who is willing to demonstrate the faith and will power to be His champion. He does not care about physical appearance, intellectual prowess or material wealth. He looks for a man or woman who is after His own heart, one of the Bible's descriptions of David.

> Now David was the son of that Ephrathite of Bethlehem Judah, whose name was Jesse, and who had eight sons. And the man was old, advanced in years, in the days of Saul. The three oldest sons of Jesse had gone to follow Saul to the battle. The names of his three sons who went to the battle were Eliab the first-born, next to him Abinadab, and the third Shammah. David was the youngest. And the three oldest followed Saul. But David occasionally went and returned from Saul to feed his father's sheep at Bethlehem.
>
> —1 SAMUEL 17:12–15, NKJV

We already looked at Goliath's stats. Now let's take a look at David's. He was about fourteen or fifteen years old and the youngest of eight brothers who helped his father with the animals. He was also an errand boy, running back and forth between the battle site and his dad's flock. But he had something going for him that was not fully realized by his father, brothers, Goliath or Samuel: David knew God.

The Lord Looks at the Heart

David had a private life that was filled with worship, honor and love for the Lord. Perhaps he nurtured that relationship during some quiet evenings tending the sheep. When Samuel came to anoint Jesse's other sons as king, all of David's siblings were rejected. David was not even with his brothers during the initial selection because he was tending the flock. But the Lord said to Samuel as he stood before Eliab, firstborn of the sons:

> Do not look at his appearance or at his physical
> stature, because I have refused him. For the Lord does
> not see as a man sees; for man looks at the outward
> appearance, but the Lord looks at the heart.
>
> —1 SAMUEL 16:7, NKJV

One by one the Lord rejected Jesse's sons until He commanded that David be brought in. When David came from tending the flock, the Lord said, "Arise, anoint him; for this is he" (1 Sam.16:12, NAS). You or I would naturally have anointed Eliab, but God saw something in David that was far more valuable than physical ability or appearance. He saw inner strength in someone who sought His will and Word. God saw a world changer in the making who would turn the world upside down.

On one of his errands to his brothers on the battle lines, David talked with some of the men when Goliath came forward with his daily challenge. David was confused by the fear he saw in the men around him and asked what would be done for the man who killed the giant. He learned that King Saul had promised a huge reward to whoever killed Goliath. Not only would the taxes of the man's father be dismissed forever, but also the person would be paid handsomely and gain the hand of one of Saul's daughters in marriage.

Characteristics of a World Impacter

This seemed like the chance of a lifetime to the young shepherd. But then his oldest brother, Eliab, accused him of being a spectator who only wanted to watch other men do battle. David defended himself and continued asking about the reward until the matter came to the attention of Saul, who sent for David. His attitude and faith exemplified the characteristics of a world impacter.

Part 2: Winning the Giant Battle

Impacters receive special rewards for exercising their faith.

> But without faith it is impossible to please Him, for he
> who comes to God must believe that He is, and that
> He is a rewarder of those who diligently seek Him.
> —HEBREWS 11:6, NKJV

How could David, who was untested in war while Goliath
was a skilled warrior, even think of challenging the enemy? He
understood an underlying principle born out of his relationship with God. *He trusted God to deliver him and fight for
him.* He had experienced God's intervention before and knew
that what God had performed once, He would perform again.
He told Saul:

> "Let no man's heart fail because of him; your servant
> will go and fight with this Philistine."
> And Saul said to David, "You are not able to go
> against this Philistine to fight with him; for you are a
> youth, and he a man of war from his youth."
> But David said to Saul, "Your servant used to keep
> his father's sheep, and when a lion or a bear came and
> took a lamb out of the flock, I went out after it and
> struck it, and delivered the lamb from its mouth; and
> when it arose against me, I caught it by its beard, and
> struck and killed it. Your servant has killed both lion
> and bear; and this uncircumcised Philistine will be
> like one of them, seeing he has defied the armies of
> the living God."
> —1 SAMUEL 17:32–36, NKJV

David had experienced God in personal struggles before. He
knew that his life was prepared for this moment, and David

believed that God would again deliver him in this new crisis. David trusted God because his faith in Him was based upon his past experiences. David's attitude exemplified the principles of a world impacter.

Impacters know and accept responsibility.

God knew that He could trust David. The young man had proven himself faithful in the little things—tending the sheep late at night when everyone else was asleep. When we prove ourselves to God, He proves Himself in us. If you are going to be a world changer, you must accept whatever responsibility, great or small, that God sets before you. No job is so small that it cannot be done responsibly before the Lord.

Impacters rely on the Lord for their strength.

David realized where his strength came from. The Lord was the one who enabled him to kill the lion and bear, and He would do the same with Goliath. Impacters know that their power comes from God.

Impacters recognize their uniqueness to God and His methods.

When Saul offered David his armor and weapons, David could not wear them because they did not fit. God had another plan for the battle.

You must recognize that God has purposely made each of us unique, with different gifts and abilities. You need to allow God to take advantage of your uniqueness for His glory. The big mistake that some Christians often make is trying to be somebody they are not. This is not only insulting to God's purpose in individual design, but it can also lead to big trouble if a person gets into the wrong ministry. God knows exactly what He is doing with us.

Part 2: Winning the Giant Battle

Principles to Be Applied

To this end, there are many principles from David that we can apply to our lives.

Remember past victories with God, and put on the full armor of God—His armor, not ours.

> Put on the whole armor of God, that you may be able to stand against the wiles of the devil.
>
> —EPHESIANS 6:11, NKJV

We need to allow God's spiritual armor to protect and keep us. *We cannot wear another person's armor because we have to maintain our own faith.* I cannot be saved by another man's faith anymore than I can be protected by another man's spiritual armor. My faith is what allows me to put the armor of God on in the first place, not someone else's.

Be prepared to do battle God's way, not man's way.

Saul tried to help David by offering his personal armor, but the shepherd boy understood that he could only fight the way God had taught him. We must do things God's way.

> There is a way that seems right to a man, but its end is the way of death.
>
> —PROVERBS 14:12, NKJV

Impacters never respond based on what "seems" right; they act upon the truth of God's Word regardless of how it might feel. Faith is action, not feeling.

Choose the basics for the battle.

David relied on the tried and true elements of his faith—not on the unproven armor of Saul. He was familiar with his sling and a few stones; anything else was unnecessary. We also must rely on the basics to fight the enemy successfully. Some basic elements of faith that we need to carry to battle against the enemy include:

- Prayer

- Worship and Bible study

- Witnessing, fellowship and servanthood

- Giving, intercession, healing, discipleship and encourage-ment

Confrontation with the enemy is inevitable.

After all the preparations are made, there comes a point when the actual conflict must occur. Usually the battle has been raging in advance in the spiritual realm before it explodes into the physical world. In fact, the confrontation began in the spiritual world when Satan foolishly thought he could usurp God's position. It has been a titanic struggle ever since, although Jesus won the ultimate conflict by going to the cross. And in the case of David, David fought Goliath without hesita-tion.

> Then he took his staff in his hand; and he chose for himself five smooth stones from the brook, and put them in a shepherd's bag, in a pouch which he had, and his sling was in his hand. And he drew near to the Philistine. So the Philistine came, and began drawing near to David, and the man who bore the shield went before him. And when the Philistine looked about and saw David, he disdained him; for he was only a youth, ruddy and good-looking. So the Philistine said to David, "Am I a dog, that you come to me with sticks?"

Part 2: Winning the Giant Battle

> And the Philistine cursed David by his gods. And the Philistine said to David, "Come to me, and I will give your flesh to the birds of the air and the beasts of the field!"
>
> —1 SAMUEL 17:40–44, NKJV

The Bible uses a very interesting word in describing Goliath's harassment of David. Scripture says he "disdained" him, which means "to disesteem or put down in ridicule." Goliath viewed David as a nonthreat and an insult to someone of his stature. Pride often blinds a person's ability to assess the strength of the opposition. Goliath used the weapons of fear, intimidation and doubt by telling David that he was a mere distraction to the main event. David, though, had other ideas.

> Then David said to the Philistine, "You come to me with a sword, with a spear, and with a javelin. But I come to you in the name of the LORD of hosts, the God of the armies of Israel, whom you have defied. This day the LORD will deliver you into my hand, and I will strike you and take your head from you. And this day I will give the carcasses of the camp of the Philistines to the birds of the air and the wild beasts of the earth, that all the earth may know that there is a God in Israel. Then all this assembly shall know that the LORD does not save with sword and spear; for the battle is the LORD'S, and He will give you into our hands."
>
> —1 SAMUEL 17:45–47, NKJV

Notice that David did not deny the reality of the problem. Instead, he named the advantages of the enemy: sword, spear and javelin. We cannot deny the power of the enemy because that would be foolish. Paul says, "We are not ignorant of his

[Satan's] schemes" (2 Cor. 2:11, NAS). Even though we are aware of the enemy's devices, it is a mistake to dwell upon them and give him glory.

There is power in the name of the Lord.

David had the greatest weapon at his disposal when it is engaged with faith: the name of the Lord (and all the authority that name represents). There is supremacy in the Lord's name:

> Therefore God also has highly exalted Him and given Him the name which is above every name, that at the name of Jesus every knee should bow, of those in heaven, and of those on earth, and of those under the earth, and that every tongue should confess that Jesus Christ is Lord, to the glory of God the Father.
> —PHILIPPIANS 2:9–11, NKJV

In one of the Gospels, Jesus said:

> In My name they will cast out demons; they will speak with new tongues; they will take up serpents; and if they drink anything deadly, it will by no means hurt them; they will lay hands on the sick, and they will recover.
> —MARK 16:17–18, NKJV

A Name Above All Others

I have personally seen the power of the name of Jesus in action. One time while I was ministering in Washington, some of my youth workers escorted a demon-possessed lady to a prayer room to do deliverance. After a short time, I went into the room, and I found a very violent girl demonstrating demonic manifestations.

The young lady rose to her feet and threatened to kill me. At that moment, I looked at the demonized girl and quoted Philippians 2:9–11. Then I said to the demon, "In Jesus' name, bow your knee." Immediately, the girl fell to her knees and could not get up again. That night I truly realized that the name of Jesus is the name above all names.

God's name brings confidence.

David had total confidence for victory in his battle with Goliath. Why? Because he fought in the name of the Lord and according to God's plan. He knew the greater outcome was not the death of a nine-foot-tall giant, but that God would be glorified. Three things happened as a result of David's obedience:

1. The world knew there was a God.

2. People realized that God does not save by carnal means.

3. Judah's world was turned upside down.

God's name brings victory.

David was as good as his prophecy. He not only knocked Goliath out with his sling, but he took the giant's sword and cut off his head. When the armies saw what had happened, there was a breakthrough for the army of Saul. The Philistines panicked and retreated into their own territory, and Israel won a mighty victory. The occupied territory was recovered, and the Philistines were humbled until another day.

Goliath's defeat shows us that:

- Victory is assured in battle if we step out in faith. God has promised us the victory if we take the risk of faith to believe His Word and call on His name. Hebrews 11 features a whole list of "faith heroes" who turned the world upside down because they believed in God for the victory.

- We must be willing to face the giants in our lives. We will go nowhere fast unless we learn that problems will not just "go away"; we must face them and dispose of them. The greater things of God often depend upon our ability to deal with the lesser problems that we all face.

- We must be willing to take a stand, even if nobody else does. David alone volunteered to fight the giant. Sometimes you may be the only one of the group who has a chance to make a difference. What will you do?

- We must focus on the Father, our victorious leader. Instead of turning to the left or right, the Bible says we are to fix "our eyes on Jesus, the author and perfecter of faith" (Heb. 12:2, NAS). Jesus must be our focus as we move ahead in faith. He is not our light at the end of the tunnel; He is our light in the tunnel.

- We must flow in the power of the Holy Spirit. It was not David's skill as a slingshot marksman that killed Goliath. The power that propelled that little stone deep into the giant's forehead was the Holy Spirit. We must partner with the Spirit of God if we are going to succeed. As we step out in faith, the Holy Spirit will enable us to be bold and speak the word of truth to whatever situation we encounter. The Bible declares, "'Not by might nor by power, but by my Spirit,' says the LORD Almighty" (Zech. 4:6). The next time you meet up with a nine-foot-nine-inch giant who thinks you are nothing but a distraction, remember that the battle belongs to the Lord.

Part 2: Winning the Giant Battle

TURNING UPSIDE DOWN

In the same way that David chose five smooth stones, write down five scriptures that you can use to attack fear when it comes to taunt you.

Chapter 11

The Fear Factor

We just learned that God's presence makes all the difference in our pursuit to turn the world upside down. Did you notice that of all the weapons at Goliath's disposal, the greatest one was fear? The Israelite army shook and quaked every time he came out and cursed them. Why? It is because they operated in fear rather than faith. When you live in faith, the devil tries to throw all kinds of insults at you. He wants to accuse and verbally abuse you so you will become frightened and give up the fight.

Maybe you have a horrible family life, or perhaps you are going through some financial hardship. Rest assured that God will never fail you if you stay in touch with Him. You need to look at your problem and say, "I don't care what it looks like. I don't care what people are saying. I am staying in faith."

God Operates in the Realm of Faith

How do we have faith? The Bible says that "faith comes by hearing, and hearing by the word of God" (Rom. 10:17, NKJV). Fear, however, can rob you of your faith and keep you from being fulfilled in the kingdom of God. It also causes you to be anxious over what your friends think or negative things that might happen in life.

In Luke 8:40–56, notice how Jesus ministered faith in an atmosphere of fear. Not only did He deal with the problem, but He also addressed the attitude surrounding the problem.

Do you see how Jesus handled it? He did not rebuke. Instead He reassuringly told Jairus to "only believe." It did not matter that people laughed at Him. He controlled the situation and acted in faith. God calls you to walk through your fears and allow Him to do an incredible ministry. So how do we operate in faith in the face of fear?

Stay in Touch With Jesus

I did not say to get a touch *from* Him, but stay in touch *with* Him. There is a big difference between *knowing* about Jesus and knowing Him. Notice how Jesus permitted only those closest to Him to enter the fearful situation with Him. With the chaotic setting, Jesus surrounded Himself only with those who were in touch with Him.

He put those without faith outside the room. I am not telling you to be rude to people who are not in agreement with you. But when you are in an atmosphere of fear, you want people around you who are filled with faith.

Quit Polluting Your Atmosphere

Much has been written about how we are killing our environment with toxic waste. Some Christians kill their witness with toxic faith. What do I mean?

- What kinds of music do you listen to?
- What types of movies do you watch?

The kind of lifestyle you live tells much about your faith. If you live a polluted, casual lifestyle, your faith will be polluted, casual and ineffective. I am not saying you have to be perfect, because that is impossible. But there are some issues about which the Spirit of God convicts you, yet you keep dumping those spiritual toxins in your life. You then wonder why God is not working in your life. Is it any wonder that so many teenagers are depressed and suicidal? It is because they live in the realm of fear and death.

In order to speak life and hope to a depressed world, you must clean up your own environment by getting rid of anything that is anti-God or impure. The world is in fear, and only people walking in faith have the answers.

Fruit Is the Result of Focus

Whatever you focus on will bear fruit. If you think about that girl or guy in immoral ways, you will find a way to bear fruit in that situation. If you are consumed by Internet pornography, you will find a way to dishonor God by visiting pornographic Web sites. The fruit is a result of the focus.

You may go to a school that is filled with challenges, including cursing, drugs and sex. It is easy to give in to these temptations, but you can hold on and not give in to them. "Fix [your] eyes upon Jesus, the author and perfecter of [your] faith" (Heb. 12:1). Jesus wants you to succeed, but you have to focus on Him.

In the Midst of a Miracle, Expect an Attack

The devil is no fool; he has been at this a long time. When he realizes that he cannot take us on head on, he will try another direction. An Old Testament story in 2 Kings 6:8–18 illustrates this really well.

Elisha was a prophet who had experienced a great number of miracles throughout Israel. Just before this incident in Dothan, he had divided a river, raised the dead and caused an iron axe head to float. Now he faced a hostile king who was jealous of Elisha's power. But in the story from 2 Kings 6, something happened in the midst of the miracle. While Elisha confronted fear with faith, the enemy struck back with a sneak attack and surrounded the city.

Just as Jesus had to deal with the enemy's laughter in Luke 8:53, Elisha had to take on the devil's assault. The attack will come, but we have to hold on to faith. Jesus told us that in this world we would face many troubles, but He also said to take heart because He already overcame everything the world can dish out. (See John 16:33.) So how do we handle the attack of the enemy?

Cultivate God's presence daily.

All of us have decisions to make that will require us to step out in faith. That is why we must cultivate God's presence in our lives daily. How? Life unfolds one day at a time, so live in God's presence daily. The music you listen to, the books you read and the friends you hang out with impact your life. But do they honor the Lord?

Expect an attack.

The devil would not be much of an enemy if he did not put up a fight. We can expect that an attack is imminent even in the midst of God working out His plan. In the story from 2 Kings 6, the Syrians surrounded the city by night. Satan specializes in sneak attacks. He wants to catch you off-guard or when you are angry or tempted. The devil wants to tear you down before you even know what is happening. We do not need to walk in fear of an attack, but we should always be ready for one.

Nothing takes God by surprise. The good news is that while we might get surprised at times, God is never taken by surprise. Notice what happened in the story. Elisha saw what was happening, but his servant was ready to panic. Instead of running, he turned to the man of faith. Whenever we hold on to faith, we need to turn to people who are operating in faith. *Remember that fear is a decision of the will. You can decide not to be afraid.*

God's angels are standing by to guard and protect us. I am not saying that we pray to or depend upon angels for our deliverance. But the Book of Hebrews tells us that there are ministering spirits sent by God to watch over those who are heirs of salvation.

There are unseen forces in the heavenly realm surrounding your life. They are unseen because their mission is not to call attention to themselves or to serve you. Their directive is to serve God, and in serving Him they also help us.

It Is Not What You See That Counts

Faith is not a matter of denying the things that are around you, but it is the greatest reality you can live in. The Bible says, "For we walk by faith, not by sight" (2 Cor. 5:7, NKJV). We have to have the attitude that no matter what we see before us, we must operate in faith. You must have the mind-set to say:

- I do not care what my friends think about me.
- I do not care if I am persecuted for my faith in school.

Develop Your Spiritual Eyesight—
the Eyes of Faith

Elisha prayed that his servant's eyes would be opened, meaning a perspective through faith. Prayer keeps the atmosphere of faith around you. The Bible speaks of things that are temporary and seen, as well as those that are eternal and unseen. (See 2 Corinthians 4:18.) When we look through the eyes of faith, we see that which is not as if it were. (See Romans 4:17.)

God Works Through Faith

Think about the most unlikely, hard-core person on your campus. What would happen if you started to "see" him through eyes of faith? What if you started praying for God to save this person to be used mightily at school? We need to come to that point where we can say, "Open my eyes, God, and let me see You at work!"

The only way you will turn your family, school, church and world upside down for God is to see them through the eyes of faith. Some of you are going to become like generals at your school—walking in God's authority and fulfilling His mission.

You need to believe and trust that He is working even if you cannot see it. God works even through difficult times. He works although the devil tries to steal your faith. How do I know? Because as illustrated in 2 Kings 6, there are more supporting you than there are against you. Do not allow the devil to steal what God has planted in your heart. I pray that your eyes will be opened afresh and anew. I pray that faith and revival will burn inside of you.

TURNING UPSIDE DOWN

1. With your natural eyes, what does your life look like?

2. With God's perspective, can you see Him working in each situation?

3. Are you putting things before your eyes or in your head that could be polluting your vision?

4. Repent, make a determination to keep your eyes on Him, and don't look back.

Chapter 12

The Power of Endurance: Keeping It Going

I have been on the subject of keeping the faith when the enemy attacks us with fear. We must walk in faith when we meet in our churches and wherever we go.

We are not hanging on out of desperation. We need to cultivate our faith because God wants to do more through us. Your friends and schools still need an outpouring of the Holy Spirit to touch them.

God desires to use you. Remember that the enemy has the façade of a roaring lion seeking whom he may devour. (See 1 Peter 5:8.) We all battle discouragement at times in our lives. We must resist the devil and his attempts to discourage us. We must remember that the cross has defeated Satan. The Bible says, "Greater is he that is in you, than he that is in the world" (1 John 4:4, KJV).

Daniel's Fight of Faith

One of the greatest examples in the Bible of a man of faith and integrity is Daniel. He had tenacious faith, as we can see demonstrated in Daniel 10:1–14.

Discouraged by what was happening to his people, Daniel mourned. They were in captivity because the enemy came in and took them all away.

Daniel was a prophet in the Old Testament whom God spoke to concerning the whole nation. A man of prayer, the Bible says in this passage that Daniel prayed twenty-one days. Do you want to see God break loose like never before in your life? What does it take for this to happen?

Make a Decision to Seek God Diligently in Prayer

If Daniel could affect the destiny of his nation, a young person can similarly affect the spiritual climate of his school, work and family through prayer. Daniel mourned and grieved because his nation was taken over by the enemy.

Are you mourning for your country? The United States is in trouble because the people have lost their way spiritually and morally. The tragedy of 9/11 should have been a wake-up call for Christians to pray to God as never before.

The devil does not play games; he goes right after you. Satan wants to destroy you and your friends, and he will do anything he can to take you out. Do you know why?

Because you belong to the greatest generation ever born. Inside you is the greatest potential to turn the world upside down for God in the present and future. The devil wants to steal, kill and destroy that before it comes out.

Satan is in full attack mode against you and me. I am a watchman, crying out to this generation to *wake up* and realize your potential. Not too long ago, I cried out to God in my living room. I said, "O God, visit this generation one more time." In Daniel 10:3, the prophet "fasted from pleasant foods." Why? Because he chose to seek God in order to bring change to his nation.

At times I have fasted for more than twenty-one days—abstaining from food partially, television and pleasurable things. I have asked the Lord to raise up a generation of young people that are so radical that they will fast from:

- Television
- Video games and movies
- The pleasures of life

We need to cry out for more of God and for less of the pleasures of the world. I pray for the passion of this book to get inside you so that you will pray like never before. Why? Kids are dying from alcohol, drugs and sex. People are dying like crazy all around us without God and hope. (See Ephesians 2:12.) If you can stand by and watch the world go to hell rather than become a person that can help turn it upside down, then something is wrong.

We can learn much from Daniel's enduring faith. His faith should be a source of encouragement to us because he was an ordinary person like you and me.

A Delay in Your Prayers Does Not Mean Denial

Daniel began to seek God, but there was a delay. He did not see an immediate answer to his prayer. Delay does not necessarily mean denial. Do not stop interceding just because your family is not saved yet. Do not give up praying just because your body is not healed yet. Do not cease believing just because the seed you have sown is not bearing fruit yet. You need to recognize by faith that it is just delayed.

Hold on to the promises of God. What has God spoken to you? You have to tell the Lord, "God, I am going to keep seeking Your face until I see the promise come into fruition." Sometimes it hurts when we do not see it happen right away. Sometimes we do not understand it, but you must never give up hope because delay is not denial.

The Message May Be Sent, but the Appointed Time Is Coming

After God has spoken and you have received the message, the appointed time may still be in the future. This means you have to hold on to faith and revival in the womb of prayer. You have to understand this principle. Some of you are so close to that breakthrough, but you are tempted to quit. Often, the more you feel like quitting, the closer the breakthrough. When God speaks, it may not always happen instantaneously, but His answer has an appointed time.

Daniel Progressed in Prayer Over Twenty-one Days

Daniel's prayer progressed in a series of steps over time. This is what kept him going until he saw the results of his prayer. Daniel 10:12 says that Daniel "set [his] heart to gain understanding." During prayer, you have to set your heart and affections to understand God. *You* have to do it because no one can jump into your skin and make it happen.

The verse also says Daniel humbled himself before God. That is a word we do not like. We do not like the word *humility*, yet that is what we need if we are going to turn our world upside down. The Bible says in James 4:6, "God resists the proud but gives grace to the humble" (NKJV). James 4:10 says to "humble yourselves in the sight of the Lord and He will lift you up" (NKJV). First Peter 5:6 says, "Therefore humble yourselves under the mighty hand of God, that He may exalt you in due time" (NKJV).

Additionally, Daniel 10:12 says that Daniel's words were heard. *Heaven responded because of one man's prayer. If we set our affections toward heaven, humble ourselves before the Lord and continue to pray, I believe heaven is going to hear and answer our prayers.*

Why don't we see things happen on our time schedule? Why isn't our environment changed immediately? It is called spiritual warfare. When you begin to pray, you are a problem to the devil. When you begin to set your face toward heaven and begin to cry out to God, all hell says, "Uh oh, we've got a live one now." Suddenly you become a threat to Satan's kingdom as you work to unseat him and turn the world upside down.

What Really Scares the Devil

The devil does not really get too scared when you praise and worship God. He does not really worry when a preacher gets up to preach. But he is terrified when God's people pray earnestly and diligently. When you pray, if you set your face toward God, humble yourself before Him and cry out to Him, you will get heaven's attention. Daniel impacted his world by prayer. That is why the devil fears the prayer meeting more than any other gathering of Christians.

My preaching is not activating things in the heavenly realm as much as my praying. I stand in the place of insignificance when I stand before men. When I pray, however, I stand in the place of significance before Almighty God.

What Held Up Daniel's Prayer?

Why was there a delay? Why didn't the Lord just deliver the message on day one and be done with it? Read Daniel 10:1–14 again, paying special attention to verses 12–13. There was a delay because there was a demon that was holding back the answer.

Delay Does Not Mean God Does Not Love You

We have to realize that God loves us. (See John 3:16.) The prophet Malachi said one of the reasons that God brought judgment to the people was because they no longer believed that He loved them. God really loves you. I do not care if you pray seven hours or one minute, it does not change God's love for you.

So what happened with Daniel's prayer? From the very first day that Daniel set his face to seek God, God heard him, and the answer was on its way. But there was such a battle in the spiritual realm that the archangel Michael had to come and kick the door open because this big demon of Persia was holding back the answer.

Many Times Demonic Opposition Delays Prayer

Do you know what the devil's strategy is? Satan thinks he can wear you out. By trying to delay God's answer to your prayers, he discourages you. However, the Bible says, "Let us not become weary in doing good, for at the proper time we will reap a harvest *if we do not give up*" (Gal. 6:9, emphasis added).

Do not become discouraged because your prayers are not answered right away. The worst thing you can do is quit praying. Do not allow a wicked, deceptive spirit to force you to give up. Do you know what we do with spirits? We rebuke them in Jesus' name and through the Holy Spirit who gives us the power to overcome.

TURNING UPSIDE DOWN

1. Describe a time in your life when your prayers were delayed.

2. How did you handle the delay?

3. Turn to the Book of James and write down scriptures on endurance and faith.

4. What lessons can you learn from Daniel, and how can you apply them to your life?

5. Like Daniel, challenge yourself for the next twenty-one days to give up something pleasurable and seek God about a specific situation in your life.

Chapter 13

The Power of Letting Go

A two-headed monster that will rob you of your faith and keep you from turning your world upside down is unforgiveness and bitterness. Many of you struggle with authority figures, perhaps your parents, teachers or pastors. Most of the counseling I do with young people deals with unforgiveness and bitterness.

Holding grudges, they tell me, "Do you know what they did to me when I was young?" I do not justify what anybody did to you. But if you do not choose to forgive—and *totally* forgive—you will be a victim for the rest of your life. Rather than turning your world upside down for Jesus, it is you who will be turned over.

Forgiveness Allows You to Continue to Move in God's Realm

Then Peter came to Him [Jesus] and said, "Lord, how often shall my brother sin against me, and I forgive him? Up to seven times?"

> Jesus said to him, "I do not say to you, up to seven times, but up to seventy times seven."
>
> —Matthew 18:21–22, nkjv

Peter did not say to Jesus, "How many times do I have to ask for forgiveness?" He asked, "When they sin against *me*, how many times do I have to forgive *them*?" Peter was focused on himself. We sometimes have that same attitude: "You are lucky that I forgive and release you from these things."

The religious institution of Peter's day said that you only had to forgive three times, and then after that you could do what you want to do. Knowing that, Peter asked, "Jesus, I have to forgive seven times, right?" Peter probably thought, *Jesus, I'm so good that I'm going to double the requirement and add one.* Peter felt proud about how many times he could forgive.

But Jesus said, "Peter, let Me teach you something. You need to forgive your brother seventy times seven." The Lord multiplied seventy times what Peter thought was good enough. Peter must have been blown out of the water. Jesus told him to forgive up to four hundred ninety times a day. Jesus made it clear that God's standard is higher than ours and cannot be accomplished in sheer human strength.

Forgiveness Requires the Holy Spirit Flowing Through You

You cannot forgive people apart from the power of God; you cannot forgive people four hundred ninety times on your own. It is not a matter of will power. Jesus wants us to come to the realization that we need to humble ourselves before God and admit that we cannot do it on our own.

When we approach God like that, He says, "I give grace to the humble, and I resist the proud. I am glad you realize you can't do it on your own, but in Me you can do it because My Spirit lives in you." Jesus taught Peter not to rely on his own strength and power. He desires to break us of the same bad habit

We Have Been Forgiven a Debt We Could Not Pay

Peter probably thought, *My goodness, I can't forgive that much.* To help Peter understand, Jesus told a parable illustrating the power of forgiving others. In the same way, you must learn from Jesus in order to forgive people so you can become more effective for God.

> Therefore the kingdom of heaven is like a certain king who wanted to settle accounts with his servants. And when he had begun to settle accounts, one was brought to him who owed him ten thousand talents [the equivalent of about a million dollars]. But as he was not able to pay, his master commanded that he be sold, with his wife and children and all he had, and that payment be made.
>
> The servant therefore fell down before him, saying, "Master, have patience with me, and I will pay you all." Then the master of that servant was moved with compassion, released him, and forgave him the debt.
>
> —MATTHEW 18:23–27, NKJV

Our Forgiveness Is More Than We Could Imagine

The servant wanted to repay the king, but the king was moved with compassion and said, "I release you. And not only do I release you from that prison sentence, but I totally wipe out your debt." How many of you would feel pretty good about that offer? Yet look at what this man does because he didn't really understand forgiveness:

> But that servant went out and found one of his fellow servants who owed him a hundred denarii [the equivalent of a few dollars]; and he laid hands on him and took him by the throat, saying, "Pay me what you owe!" So his fellow servant fell down at his feet and begged him, saying, "Have patience with me, and I will pay you all." And he would not, but went and threw him into prison till he should pay the debt.
>
> —MATTHEW 18:28–30, NKJV

The servant was not thinking straight. If I was forgiven a million-dollar debt and prison sentence, what should I do to this guy that owed me the equivalent of a few dollars? This man was so enraged and angry that he threw the borrower into prison until he could pay the debt.

Why would the servant, who represents you and me, want to get a couple of bucks from somebody when he just had his million-dollar debt pardoned? I believe that in the back of his mind, he thought he would have to repay that money. So, he sought the money to pay the king back for what he owed, even though the king had wiped out his debts.

The Bible says that when his fellow servants saw what he had done, they were very grieved and told their master what happened. The servant did not know that there were people watching him. Likewise, somebody is watching you. You may think that you are getting away with something, but you are deceiving yourself.

Proverbs 15:3 says, "The eyes of the LORD are everywhere,

keeping watch on the wicked and the good." The Bible says the eyes of the Lord are watching everything, observing the good and evil. Some of you think you are sly, getting away with something that your mom and dad told you not to do. But God is watching you!

Our Sin Matters to God, and It Hurts Him

When God sees you doing things you should not be doing, His first response is to be grieved, and He hurts and feels pain. But God does not want to inflict judgment on you. Why does God grieve? I believe He realizes that sin, especially unforgiveness, is only going to hurt you. God has a heart of compassion and one of a loving father toward you.

> So when his fellow servants saw what had been done, they were very grieved, and came and told their master all that had been done. Then his master, after he had called him, said to him, "You wicked servant! I forgave you all the debt because you begged me."
>
> —MATTHEW 18:31–32, NKJV

How much has God forgiven you and me? How many times have we come to God asking forgiveness for the same thing because we blew it again? If God treated us as we treated each other, I do not think any of us would be alive.

Angry and upset, the king told the servant:

> "Should you not also have had compassion on your fellow servant, just as I had pity on you?" And his master was angry, and delivered him to the torturers until he should pay all that was due to him.
>
> —MATTHEW 18:33–34, NKJV

Overwhelmed, the king did not understand why the servant could not forgive a few dollars. What am I saying about God the Father? God understands everything, yet a part of Him says, "Don't they get it yet? How much have I forgiven them, but they are caught up in a little-bitty offense that will rob them of faith and revival. Because they do not fully understand My forgiveness, I now have to judge them." The king first gave grace and mercy to the servant. In the same manner, if we do not learn from grace and mercy, judgment will come. Grace and mercy give us heaven, but judgment will give us hell.

Unforgiveness Kills Your Faith and Leads to Torment

If you do not choose to forgive, your faith will be wiped out. Additionally, unforgiveness will torment you until you forgive. Some of you may have been abused and hurt, which causes you to hold a grudge. Your bitterness and anger torment you. When you have unforgiveness, Jesus says you are like the wicked servant who would not forgive the little bit of money, even though God forgave his debt that he could not pay. God is not going to torment you, but you have opened yourself up to torment because of unforgiveness.

Maybe Jesus' biggest point in the story comes in Matthew 18:35 (NKJV) when He says:

> So My heavenly Father also will do to you if each of you, from his heart, does not forgive his brother his trespasses.

If you have bitterness and unforgiveness in your heart and you ask God to forgive you, He does not even hear you.

Do you know why there is no forgiveness for those who harbor bitterness and unforgiveness? It is because they do not really understand God's forgiveness. You and I deserve death and hell because we have sinned, but Jesus has paid the penalty of our sins. Without forgiveness, there is no salvation. When you do not have forgiveness, your relationship with God is hindered. You need to choose to forgive. Forgiveness is not a feeling; it is a choice.

TURNING UPSIDE DOWN

1. Do you have trouble with forgiveness?

2. Is there somebody right now that you need to forgive?

3. Write out a list of people that you have not forgiven.

4. Begin to pray and decide to forgive each one individually on your list.

5. Realize how much God has forgiven you and rejoice.

Chapter 14

The Reality of Hell

From the most primitive tribes in unexplored jungles to the streets of New York City, there is one common destiny that awaits us: death. Whether we are black, white, rich or poor, God has appointed a definite number of days for us to enjoy an earthly life. If Jesus delays His return, everyone reading this book will take their last breath on earth.

At some point, we all face that final step where we leave this life and move into the next phase. For many, death evokes great fear and mystery, while others have sought to deal with it through various "pathways" of spirituality. This chapter is a warning of the impending danger that will come whether you are nineteen or ninety-nine. The world is dying to hear this truth: Hell is real and very hungry.

The biggest deception the devil has sold to the world is the lie that there is a heaven, but there is no hell. Some of you are on a collision course with hell, and someone must warn you about it. That is right. There are some reading this book who have not yet asked Jesus to become their Savior and Lord. Perhaps you believe you will go to heaven, but unless you deal with your heart, you may be in for a big shock. It is a tragic deception if you think you are heavenbound because you are a good person or a regular churchgoer.

The Follics of the Rich Man

The rich man in Luke 16:19-31 had it made. He wore the latest fashions, ate the best gourmet foods and had everything he wanted. Do you know anybody like that? They get everything they want and, like the rich man, have everything this life can offer.

It is not bad for you to have money and things, but it is not good for possessions to possess you.

I do not advocate a "poor" mentality. If I were poor, I could not help people who need money. God is not against riches, but He is against riches having you. The Bible says in 1 Timothy 6:10 that "the love of money is a root of all kinds of evil." God wants to bless us so we can be a blessing. We can, however, be consumed with God's blessings.

The Faith of Lazarus

Lazarus the beggar sat at the rich man's house every day. All the beggar desired was to eat of the remains from the rich man's table.

In those days, when they washed their hands, they took loaves of bread to wipe their hands clean. The loaves of bread would then be thrown away.[1] The rich man was so stingy and caught up into his riches that he would not even give Lazarus the bread that he cleaned his hands with.

The Bible questions the quality of our love when we do not share with others, especially another brother or sister in Christ.

How we handle our material possessions will tell us how much we really love others.

> This is how we know what love is: Jesus Christ laid down his life for us. And we ought to lay down our lives for our brothers. If anyone has material possessions and sees his brother in need but has no pity on him, how can the love of God be in him?
>
> —1 JOHN 3:16–17

Everything was great for the rich man—until he died. Death is the final equalizer; it makes everybody even. Death is no respecter of persons. What happens after death? Do you know where you are going?

The Reality of Hell

In Luke 16:23, the rich man found himself in hell. If you are not a Christian and you die right now, you will go to a place called hell, a place prepared for the devil, not man. It exists, despite what New Age and other religions say. Hell is a holding tank until the final judgment. Everyone who has ever died without knowing Jesus—from the greatest villains in history to some of the nicest people you ever knew—are now there awaiting their final judgment. (See Revelation 20:11–15.)

It is a place where people are aware of who they were in life. In hell, people know the choices and mistakes they made. In torment, they await an even greater terror in the lake of fire.

In the story of the rich man, Lazarus was in heaven, but the rich man was in torment in hell. The word *torment* means physical pain, anguish, vexation or pain beyond your imagination. The rich man was fully conscious; he knew what was happening to him. Not only that—he had the form of a body.

You may think we are going to be some spirit matter after this life. In heaven we will have glorified bodies, while those in hell will have the form of a body with real sensations. The rich man said he was in torment and pain.

> Then He will also say to those on the left hand, "Depart from Me, you cursed, into the everlasting fire prepared for the devil and his angels…" And these will go away into everlasting punishment.
>
> —MATTHEW 25:41, 46, NKJV

Notice that the punishment will last forever. The torment lasts not just night and day, but forever. Whether you believe this is or not, the Bible says these things will happen.

Playing With Eternity Like It Is a Game

Some of you treat eternity like a coin toss. You play a chance game with God: If it is heads, I will serve God, but if it is tails, I will not. However, eternity is not something to play with. Jesus said:

> If your hand causes you to sin, cut it off. It is better for you to enter into life maimed, rather than having two hands, to go to hell, into the fire that shall never be quenched—where "their worm does not die and the fire is not quenched." And if your foot causes you to sin, cut it off. It is better for you to enter life lame, rather than having two feet, to be cast into hell…And if your eye causes you to sin, pluck it out. It is better for you to enter the kingdom of God with one eye, rather than having two eyes, to be cast into hell fire—where "their worm does not die and the fire is not quenched."
>
> —MARK 9:43–48, NKJV

Jesus does not encourage you to cut off your hand, but He warns you to get rid of everything that would keep you from heaven.

Some of you need to sever worldly and ungodly relationships, perhaps even with your best friend. Are you going to risk your life for eternity?

You know what really prevented me from having sex and doing drugs? It was a fear of hell. Proverbs tells us that the fear of the Lord is the beginning of wisdom.

Why would you throw away your whole life for something that is temporary? The Bible says, "No eye has seen, no ear has heard…what God has prepared for those who love him" (1 Cor. 2:9). Momentary pleasures are not worth eternal damnation.

The Rich Man's Greatest Torment: He Saw What He Missed

He was able to see what he had missed out on. Do you know hell's greatest torment? It is not the pain, but the total separation from the presence of God. Going to hell means you can never again feel everything that God has for you. The rich man never had a second chance once he was in hell.

Once We Enter Eternity, Our Destination Is Forever

In Luke 16:26, Abraham says, "And besides all this, between us and you there is a great gulf fixed, so that those who want to pass from here to you cannot, nor can those from there pass to us" (NKJV). In other words, once your eternal destiny is set, there is no turning back—no second chances. It is done.

The rich man knew that his destination was final, but notice what he said:

I beg you therefore, father, that you would send him [Lazarus] to my father's house, for I have five brothers, that he may testify to them, lest they also come to this place of torment.

—LUKE 16:27–28, NKJV

Take Every Opportunity to Listen to God's Word

I realize that many of you reading this book are on fire for God, living in the Lord's power and want to turn your world upside down. However, some of you who are reading this book need to take a real close look at your lives.

There are two destinations. *You are either on the road to heaven or on a highway to hell. There is no road in between, and the paths go in opposite directions. So you cannot say you are on the road to heaven unless you are walking according to God's will and His Word. Your eternal destiny is reflected in your lifestyle.*

Jesus said:

No servant can serve two masters; for either he will hate the one and love the other, or else he will be loyal to the one and despise the other. You cannot serve God and mammon.

—LUKE 16:13, NKJV

Choose this day to serve Jesus with all your heart, and never turn back.

TURNING UPSIDE DOWN

1. What was your vision of hell before this chapter?

2. Have there been times when you rejected the opportunity to hear the gospel?

3. Write down a list of at least three people you know that are on the road to hell without divine intervention. Now pray for them. Ask God also for opportunities to share the Lord with them and for these people to be receptive to the gospel.

SECTION THREE

Upside-Down Activity

Jesus always taught that hearing His words was not enough. A wise man hears God's Word, then does something with it. So what are we supposed to do? Let's take some basic ideas, which result in a world turned upside down.

Chapter 15

Praying With Power

Prayer. The very word creates a number of thoughts. To some, it means a time alone with the Father or just a few words spoken before dinner. To others, it is something rarely done because they do not know how to pray or are not sure what it is all about. But to those who want to turn the world upside down, it is the power of God released in their lives.

Are you ready to see people healed and circumstances turned around? Are you ready to see the world around you turned upside down for Christ? It will not happen if you are not praying.

Four Types of Prayer

The Book of James outlines four types of prayer for a world changer.

> Is any one of you in trouble? He should pray. Is anyone happy? Let him sing songs of praise. Is any one of you sick? He should call the elders of the church to pray over him and anoint him with oil in the name of the Lord. And the prayer offered in faith will make the sick person well; the Lord will raise him up. If he has sinned, he will be forgiven. Therefore

confess your sins to each other and pray for each other so that you may be healed. The prayer of a righteous man is powerful and effective.

Elijah was a man just like us. He prayed earnestly that it would not rain, and it did not rain on the land for three and a half years. Again he prayed, and the heavens gave rain, and the earth produced its crops.

—James 5:13–18

Personal prayer

James 5:13 says, "Is any one of you in trouble? He should pray." The emphasis is on you and me. *The Bible says that if you are in trouble, you should pray. It is a personal responsibility.* We do not like that in America though. It is easier to blame someone else. If you are in trouble, the Bible does not say for you to call the pastor, your friend or parents first. God's Word says you should pray.

Corporate prayer

James 5:14–15 commands us that if anyone is sick, he should call for the elders. The Bible says if you are sick, YOU should call. It says you should call for the elders of the church. Then they should come, lay hands on you and anoint you with oil in the name of the Lord. What happens after that? You believe with all your heart that you will be healed.

I have testimonies of a lady who had a left arm and left leg grow out instantaneously after she was prayed for. We had a kid who had a broken collarbone that snapped right back into place. We had another lady who had a growth on her female organs. After we prayed for her, the power of God hit her, and she became well immediately. She went to the doctor the next day, and her physician said a biopsy was not even needed because all of her cells were normal.

What am I saying? The prayer of faith works. Do you want to know how to build your faith? By hearing the Word of God. (See Romans 10:17.) You get faith by communing with God's Word and by praying and seeking His face.

Partner prayer

James 5:16 says, "Therefore confess your sins to each other and pray for each other so that you may be healed." Notice it says we must first confess our sins, which means that we must admit that we are wrong. When you are wrong, you are wrong. When you have done something wrong, and you finally confess it, you feel so much better after you get it off your chest.

Some of you do not have a clear conscience and are walking around under a cloud of guilt as you read these words. You cannot sleep well at night; you cannot get a breakthrough in your life because you have unconfessed sin in your life. The Bible says that if we regard iniquity in our heart, God does not even hear us. (See Isaiah 59:2.) The word *regard* means "know about, cherish and hold on to."

You believe God is graceful and merciful—He is—and that He loves you—He does. But if you regard sin in your heart, He does not even hear you.

> If my people, who are called by my name, will humble themselves and pray and seek my face and turn from their wicked ways, then will I hear from heaven and will forgive their sin and will heal their land.
>
> —2 Chronicles 7:14

Do you think the ungodly are going to respond to God? They are lost in a world turned upside down by Satan. The only people capable of responding to God are His children. If Christians will repent of their sins, God will turn and heal this nation.

Passionate prayer

James 5:16 says, "The effectual fervent prayer of a right-eous man availeth much" (KJV). *Effectual* means "effective or brings about results." *Fervent* means "hanging on, showing great intensity of spirit, hot, burning, growing to a boil and passionate." Elijah is an example of a man of passionate prayer.

Elijah—Man of Passion

The Bible says very clearly that Elijah was a man like us. He was a man with struggles, fears and doubts. That makes me feel good. God is not looking for you to be Superman. He does not want you to be something that you are not. God desires for you to be real. He knows that you have struggles and that you have things in your life.

If God can use Elijah, God can use you. Why? He can use you because God is looking for ordinary people to do extraor-dinary things. So what is He looking for? He is looking for you just to yield to Him and say, "God, use me." When you say this and sincerely mean it, God will use you.

Elijah was a man just like us.

Elijah was a man with the same passions and desires that we have. Elijah did one thing that I love—he *prayed.* Prayer was the lifeblood of Elijah. If you are a person of prayer, you will be a person of power and influence. People will flock around you to ask questions about God.

Why? It is because you know God, and you cannot know the Lord unless you talk to Him. Elijah talked with Him, calling upon God earnestly. He prayed with fervency and per-severance.

Elijah's prayers impacted the world and his life.

How do you know if your prayer is fervent, effectual and really making a difference? When you pray with fervency and passion, you are affected. God looks not just for people to impact the world, but He seeks those who will be changed on the inside. True prayer is birthed in the heart of God.

When you get alone with God and pray for things on the outside, God will deal with things inside you as He speaks to you. Everybody wants to affect the world, but true men and women of God are also changed on the inside.

Elijah prayed earnestly for the atmosphere to be changed.

Elijah prayed earnestly that it would not rain. In 1 Kings 17:1, the Bible says the Word of the Lord came to him and said to pray that the heavens and the atmosphere would be stopped. Your prayers are changing the spiritual atmosphere when they are fervent and passionate. Just as the rain stopped, I believe the demonic downpour in our world will be stopped and dried up in Jesus' mighty name. But it will not happen if we do not pray.

God looks for us to pray. We need to stand in the gap and say, "God, if nobody else is going to pray in this state, I will pray, seek Your face and call upon heaven so You can change the spiritual climate of the land."

Elijah prayed for physical and spiritual rain.

In 1 Kings 18:41–46, Elijah prayed seven times, and the rain returned. What is special about rain? Many times it is symbolic of revival. (See Joel 2:28–29.) Rain brings refreshing and new life. What stops the rain? Rain is stopped by the sin of God's people. (See 2 Chronicles 6:26–27; 7:13–14.)

Elijah got on his knees before the Lord.

When Elijah knelt before God, it was a sign of surrender and humility. In the Hebrew text, the Bible says he was in an agonizing position. He travailed and cried out to the Lord, but he didn't see rain. Although he prayed fervently, nothing happened until he called on God a seventh time.

Some of you give up too easily. When your prayer is not answered right away, you give up and lose faith. How do you hold on to faith and revival with an attitude like that? After Elijah prayed a seventh time, he told his servant Gehazi to check the sky for rain. A surprised Gehazi said, "A cloud as small as a man's hand is rising from the sea." (See 1 Kings 18:44.)

In the realm of prayer, you need to see just a little glimmer of light and hope that says God is moving. Why do I say God is moving? Because like Gehazi, I see a cloud the size of a man's hand as you pray earnestly. You do not need a big sign; you just need a little crack in the door.

Why are you reading this book right now? I do not think it is because you have it all together. It is because you see a cloud the size of a man's hand, and you see revival coming. In the story of Elijah, one man's prayers changed the atmosphere, turning his world upside down.

Can the same thing happen today with more than one person praying? Certainly, one man can change a nation. For you, your nation is your school, workplace and home.

Elijah got up and ran faster than a chariot.

> The seventh time the servant reported, "A cloud as small as a man's hand is rising from the sea. So Elijah said, "Go and tell Ahab, 'Hitch up your chariot and go down before the rain stops you.'" Meanwhile, the sky grew black with clouds, the wind rose, a heavy rain

came on and Ahab rode off to Jezreel. The power of the LORD came upon Elijah and, tucking his cloak into his belt, he ran ahead of Ahab all the way to Jezreel.
—1 KINGS 18:44–46

In verse 46, what was the significance of Elijah running faster than the chariot? Power only comes through prayer. God enables you to do things you do not even think you could do. You may not run fast and take the state track championship, but you can be as bold as a lion and witness to people to whom you have never witnessed. Through God's power, you will lay hands on people at school and see them healed. Like Elijah who prayed and saw results, you see the cloud the size of a man's hand. If you want faith and revival to continue in your life so you can turn the world upside down, you have to pray.

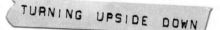

TURNING UPSIDE DOWN

1. What does your prayer life consist of?

2. Take some time right now and write out a commitment to personal daily prayer.

3. Jesus gave us this outline in Matthew 6:9–13 (NKJV):

Our Father in heaven, hallowed be Your name.

Start praying by magnifying God and thanking Him.

Your Kingdom come. Your will be done on earth as it is in heaven.

Ask God for His will to be done in every situation of your life and for others.

Give us this day our daily bread.

Ask Him for His provision for you, your family and friends.

And forgive us our debts, as we forgive our debtors.

Choose to forgive, not holding on to bitterness and unforgiveness. Remember how much you have been forgiven.

And do not lead us into temptation, but deliver us from the evil one.

Admit that you cannot do it on your own; rely on God's help.

For Yours is the kingdom and the power and the glory forever.

Remember that God is on the throne. You can trust Him with every detail of your life.

Chapter 16

The Weapon of Worship

Praise and worship are not just a ritualistic task of the modern church service. Praise and worship are not just ideas that someone made up thousands of years ago for the sake of filling time. Praise and worship go back even before there was an earth. Praise and worship are timeless because they originated in heaven before the creation of the world. Praise and worship will continue even after the creation of a new heaven and earth. (See Revelation 21:1.)

In heaven there is no preaching; there is no witnessing. In heaven there is only praise and worship.

The angels go back and forth over God's throne, saying, "Holy, holy, holy is the Lord" (Rev. 4:8). The passage also says that the elders around the throne lay their crowns down, bowing and worshiping God. (See Revelation 4:10.) The reason the angels and elders can forever worship God is that each time they bow and again raise their eyes, they behold a new facet of His majesty. So overwhelmed by His glory, the company falls forward on their faces, crying, "Holy, holy, holy is the Lord."

The Weapon of Worship

This is a powerful example of what worship accomplishes for us. When we take the time to focus on Him and truly worship Him, the eyes of our understanding are opened, and we see Him in His glory. During a time of worship is when the Lord is enabled to show us more fully His infinite ability.

Do you have a situation in which you need divine help? Worship Him, and let the Lord show you the answer for the circumstance. I can guarantee you will be overwhelmed by His glory and goodness. Let the Lord speak to you in your time of worship. Let Him refresh you in His presence. Let Him fill you with strength to face every situation in your life right now.

The Power of Worship

Worship is a powerful weapon. The devil does not want you to adore God because he understands that a person of praise and worship is a person of power. The Bible says that death and life are in the power of the tongue. (See Proverbs 18:21.) What you speak is very important. As we worship, we naturally shift our attention off ourselves and onto the Lord. We are Christians; we have an advantage. We do not have to go through our lives by ourselves. We have supernatural intervention. Worship takes our eyes from the situation to the solution, from the problem to the Provider, from the cares of this world to the constant love of the Father.

People of Praise Are People of Power

In our worship time, our eyes are opened, and we are in a posture to hear clearly His direction. Instead of looking down on earthly circumstances, we are redirected to Jesus. Our perspective is changed, and we remember, "God is still on the throne, and He is in control. God is all-powerful, all-knowing and all-good, and we're going to be OK."

In my own life, when a situation seems overwhelming, I praise and worship God. As we sing songs of His love, His grace, His mercy and His miracles, we cannot help but be encouraged and renewed.

Complaining Hinders Praise and Power

A major hindrance to a move of God's power in our lives is complaining. The Bible says that the children of Israel consistently complained, "We want manna. We want bread. We want meat."

Complaining opens us up to the attack of the devil. In the Old Testament, serpents bit the people because they complained. (See Numbers 21:6.) And of course, complaining does not make your situation any better. Instead of reaping the manifest power of God, you reap the opposite.

Try praising the Lord the next time you find yourself in a situation that seems unfair or overwhelming.

> *Thank You, Lord, for who You are. I bless You for Your goodness. You are my shelter, strong tower and my very present help in time of need.*

The devil will eventually take notice that you cannot be deterred from worshiping God. Imagine the e-mail forwarded through all of hell:

> Memo to All Demons:
> Leave _[insert your name]_ alone because the more we hassle him [or her], the more he [or she] praises God.
>
> —Satan

God Is a Holy God

> But You are holy, enthroned in the praises of Israel.
> —Psalm 22:3, nkjv

The psalmist said, "You are a holy God!" When we worship, we need to understand whom we are worshiping. The Bible says that God is holy, which means He is pure and perfect—unlike fallen man. He is unadulterated. There is no sin in His life. God's character is unblemished because He is holy. Because of His holiness, we can always trust that His motives are pure. We never have to worry about asking for His will to be done; His holiness ensures that His will is perfect in every circumstance.

Why Should We Worship?

The psalmist declared, "God, You are not only holy, but also you are enthroned in the praises of Israel." (See Psalm 22:3.) He is talking about our praise and worship!

Our praise and worship create a throne where God can get comfortable. The word *enthroned* or *inhabit* means "to sit down, to remain, to settle or to literally come and be married to." No matter what situation you face, when you praise and worship God, you are building a throne for Him to sit on, settle into and remain in your life and that particular area.

Jack Hayford has said:

> The word *enthroned* indicates that wherever God's people exalt His name, He is ready to manifest His kingdom's power in the way most appropriate to the situation.[1]

Praise creates an entry point for God's kingdom to come in and His will to be done in human circumstances.

What kind of throne would be built if everybody worshiped like you? Would God be sitting on an apple crate or on a magnificent throne? I do not know about you, but I want to build Him a throne that is worthy of a king. Keep this in mind the next time you do not feel like worshiping God.

Not only do our praise and worship create a throne for God, but our praise and worship are gifts of true value that we can give to a God who has everything. What else do you give a God who owns all the silver and gold, or a God who owns the whole earth? He longs for you to give Him praise and offer Him worship. In doing this, you are offering yourself!

If we do not do it, the very rocks will cry out. (See Luke 19:40.) We serve an awesome God; He is unsurpassed in greatness. I want to build Him a bigger throne and a bigger entry point for His manifest presence and glory in my life.

When we sing praises and worship the Lord, the windows of heaven are opened wider and wider for God to establish His kingdom in the situations that we face. He will inhabit the throne that we build. Your praise and worship can build a throne that is bigger than the mountain in your way. So when God sits down on the throne of praise and worship, that mountain is nothing because we serve a God with whom all things are possible.

The Tangible Power of Praise and Worship

Praise and worship release the tangible power of God to change your situation. In 2 Chronicles 20, the Bible says that King Jehoshaphat was surrounded by the enemy, so he fasted and prayed. God then gave him a simple strategy through the prophets.

- Jehoshaphat was told not to fear or worry because the battle was not his, but God's. Aren't you glad that God is in control?

- Jehoshaphat did not get anxious. He told the people, "Israel, don't worry about this. God is going before us; we will have victory. We're going to go out there, and God is going to fight on our behalf."

Everyone was excited. Everyone, including the army, was ready, but then Jehoshaphat told them, "We have one change in our strategy."

"All the Worshipers Go First"

Jehoshaphat appointed the praise and worship team to lead in front of the army before they went to battle. Members of the choir and orchestra probably said, "Wait a second, Jehoshaphat. They have swords, bows and arrows. We don't have any weapons. The army should go first."

The king wanted the worshipers to go first because Jehoshaphat knew God promised them victory. In the same way, if we send out worshipers to exalt God, the throne will be built, and His glory will come. His kingdom will also be established, and we will see victory in our lives. So Jehoshaphat's people began to worship, and the Bible says that as they worshiped, the enemy turned upon themselves. Praise and worship confuse and freak out the devil.

Did you know that most scholars believe that at one time the devil was the worship leader in heaven? Can you imagine leading worship in heaven for God but getting kicked out because of rebellion? The devil hates to hear worship because he wanted to be worshiped. Lucifer, or Satan, said, "I will exalt my throne [in the heavens]…I will be like the Most High" (Isa. 14:13-14, NKJV).

Will You Be Like Jehoshaphat?

Some of you may say, "What does Jehoshaphat have to do with me? Jehoshaphat didn't have bills. Jehoshaphat didn't have family or relationship struggles in marriage. Jehoshaphat wasn't trying to live a pure life in an impure culture." He probably did not face those situations, but he knew that praise and worship were the key to victory in life's battles.

Praising God Releases His Power in Your Situation

Remember Paul and Silas's situation from Acts 16:25–36? They were beaten in prison, then placed in the inner dungeon. It was not like a prison in America today. They did not have a cafeteria, bunk bed, commode, air conditioning or heat. But the Bible says that at midnight they did two things:

- They worshiped and praised God.
- They prayed.

In the midst of their bleak circumstances, they worshiped God because He is holy and worthy. They worshiped God because they knew that their praise would build a throne for God to inhabit.

The Bible says that as they sang and praised God, the other prisoners listened. They probably said to one another, "Who are the two new prisoners? Don't they know this is a prison? Don't they know you don't worship when you're in these circumstances? Don't they know that they messed up? There's no way out."

The Weapon of Worship

Paul and Silas were not like the other prisoners because they knew that the jail walls, steel bars and chains could not hold their spirits. Their spirit man instinctively cried out to God because they knew He could save them.

You cannot be strapped down by your circumstances because you are a spiritual being having a temporary human experience. You are not a human being having a temporary spiritual experience. You have to train your spirit man to worship God because it will live longer than your flesh.

As Paul and Silas praised and worshiped God, their praise and worship caught the other prisoners' attention. Who is listening to you at your job? If there is a possible layoff and fellow employees worry, what will your reaction be? Your school, friends and neighborhood are paying attention to see and hear what kind of a Christian you are in good and bad times.

Praising God releases His power in your situation.

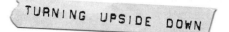

TURNING UPSIDE DOWN

1. What areas should you be praising God about instead of complaining?

2. What kind of throne have you built God for these situations?

3. For each one of these issues, find a scripture on praise and write it down.

4. The next time a complaint comes to mind, replace it with the Word. Build a great throne for the Lord to come and dwell in the midst of your circumstances.

Chapter 17

An Upside-Down Commission

They are some of the cleanest-cut, nicest-looking young men you have ever seen. They always sport a white shirt and tie. Sometimes they don Oakleys and listen to music on their headsets as they ride their bikes in pairs in your neighborhood. They are sincere in their mission for the Church of Jesus Christ of Latter-Day Saints. They are out to turn the world upside down for the cause of Mormonism—and they are doing a pretty good job.

Rise of Spiritual Alternatives

Christianity used to dominate the culture in the United States. But that time has long passed. Instead, spirituality in a variety of forms seems to be on the rise. Everything from classic cults to New Age is competing for attention. Did you known Islam is one of the fastest-growing religions in the United States today?

If there was ever a time for disciples of Jesus Christ to be committed to preaching the gospel, it is now. We have to be true to our commitment to Jesus to turn our world upside down for Him. It is your generation who must raise the banner of Christ over this society, which has slipped into cultic heresy and religious bondage.

Salt of the Earth

In Matthew 5:13, Jesus told us that we are to be the "salt of the earth." What does that mean? It means we need to stand out and be different from all the other religions and spirituality that people are buying into. It means we must have something to offer other than just another religion.

Recently, I was in a drive-thru burger place called In-and-Out. I ordered my favorite burger and fries. As I pulled to the window, I was asked if I wanted salt for my fries. I tossed the packet into the bag and drove off. As I ate the fries, I noticed that they were definitely bland, so I found the packet and poured salt on the fries. Now the fries tasted great. The salt was potent, but until it was released from its container, it was not effective.

This is what Jesus was talking about in Matthew 5. He tells us that we are the salt of the earth. We have to be spilled out and used in order to be effective. In the ancient world, salt was highly valued and was important in three main areas:

1. *Purity.* The Romans thought salt was the purest of all elements. The origin of salt was the sun and the sea— two of nature's greatest and most pure elements. Jesus said that we as Christians must be pure, too.

2. *Preservative.* In the ancient world, salt was used to preserve food. Since there was no modern refrigeration in those days, food could easily spoil. Salt had a way of keeping meat from rotting. It is the same way

for Christians. We are called to be a preservative of God's grace in society. Our lives reflect the grace of the living God.

3. *Flavor.* Salt demonstrates the richness of food. As Christians, we need to show the world that the Christian life is rich, rewarding and "tastes good." The world should look at us and say, "How can their lives be so filled with flavor?" When was the last time an unbeliever was envious of your life? Jesus made it clear that He came to give us abundant life. (See John 10:10.) As salt, we have been set apart from the rest of the world, but we are supposed to flavor our world with Christ.

But how can we be salt to a world that does not want to be salted? This can only happen if the church begins to evangelize with the same passion and intensity that groups like the Mormons possess. There is, however, a major difference: *The passion and intensity of the world will never take the place of the power of the Holy Spirit working through us.* The world can be won to Jesus one person at a time because we have the power of God with us.

Evangelism

Evangelism is an interesting word. It is a Greek compound of two ideas: *ev*, which means "good," and *angel*, which means "message."

Evangelism is the delivery of the "evangel"—the Good News of Jesus' salvation. All of God's children are called to spread the Good News. I do not care if it is not your gift, whether you are shy or are scared to death to share your faith. You had better figure out a way to be a messenger for Christ, or your world will never be turned upside down.

Latter-Day Competition

From its first days, the Christian church has had to deal with false teachings that attacked the church from within and on the outside. Paul had to fight some of these heresies in his writings. The Bible warns us that we are to be strong in our faith and sure of what we believe, especially in light of these religious contenders.

The following statements urge us to be on guard:

- Do not be carried away by strange teachings. (See Hebrews 13:9.)

- Some will depart from the faith in latter times. (See 1 Timothy 4:1.)

- Itching ears will be satisfied with unholy doctrines. (See 2 Timothy 4:3–5.)

All of these refer to a point in time when people will search for God through various ways and places—everywhere except in His Holy Word. Do you see that search today on your campus and at your job? People know they need hope, but they look everywhere except in the right place. Do you see why this world needs to be turned upside down?

This is happening now. We know the world is slipping into satanic deception. The Bible predicted it, but what did Paul say that we should do about it? Here is a word of encouragement from a man who faced hellish trials for the sake of the gospel:

> But you be watchful in all things, endure afflictions,
> do the work of an evangelist, fulfill your ministry.
> —2 TIMOTHY 4:5, NKJV

The Great Commission

Did you know that God has entrusted you with the greatest information in the history of the universe? You and I are called to be the communicators of a message of hope, freedom, deliverance and destiny. The Great Commission comes out of the Book of Matthew. At the very end of the book, Jesus tells his followers what their mission is.

> Then Jesus came to them and said, "All authority in heaven and on earth has been given to me. Therefore go and make disciples of all nations, baptizing them in the name of the Father and of the Son and of the Holy Spirit, and teaching them to obey everything I have commanded you. And surely I am with you always, to the very end of the age."
>
> —MATTHEW 28:18–20

Notice that this is not a request. It is a command. If we are not actively involved in making disciples and partnering with the Holy Spirit to see people won to Jesus, then we are being disobedient to the Lord. Let's take a look at the elements of this process:

The commissioner

Jesus Christ is the one who is commissioning. All authority has been given to Him, and He allows us to piggyback on that authority so we can be effective. Jesus commands you to win your campus, friends and family to Him.

The commission

It means evangelizing the world. Does this mean you have to go to Africa or Brazil? No, but it does mean that you have been assigned a strategic mission field of your own. For some it may be a foreign land; for most, however, it's your neighborhood, school and workplace. Did you know there are some people that only YOU have any influence over? Start working your mission field.

The components

Make disciples. The bottom line of the Great Commission is to make disciples. This means getting people saved through the power of the Holy Spirit. It is not up to you to save them, but it is up to you to bring them the Good News. It is also your responsibility to pray for them and be there for them when you can. What is a disciple? It is someone who is faithful, available and teachable. Our job is to make students of the lost so that they will learn about Jesus.

Baptizing in water. This is a mark of a disciple. Water baptism confirms the work that God is doing. It is not a magic potion, and the water does not save you. But God wants us to be baptized in water to show that we are really His. Have you been baptized in water yet? What is keeping you?

Teaching. After people become disciples and move toward baptism, they must be taught the truth of God's Word. It is important to buy them a Bible, get them into a Bible-believing church and give them tapes of good preachers. It is also wise to teach them faith. Do whatever you can so the new believer gets taught and established in the Word of God.

Jesus promised that as we do all these things, He will always be with us. His presence is alive in the midst of His commission. Jesus drives and gives authority for the Great Commission. With the same authority that He gave us over demons and devils, He enables us to go and win our friends and family. You have authority to turn the world upside down.

As disciples, we have to be in the business of evangelism. There is no way around it. By definition, a good disciple follows the instructions of his teacher. Our teacher has commanded that we teach others. The mission can only be accomplished through your willingness to go, empowered by the Holy Spirit working through you.

TURNING UPSIDE DOWN

1. Think of two examples in your own life where you were the flavor of God, salt and light to others. Perhaps you stood your ground in a compromising situation, or you were courteous and respectful to your teachers.

2. Imagine that you had not acted in a Christlike manner in those situations. What impact do you think would have been made on those around you? What kind of an evangelist would you have been?

3. Are you walking out your faith daily by being a witness in your actions and not just your words?

4. Are you plugged into a youth church and actively pursuing knowledge in God's Word? Are you committed to attending church weekly? Have you been baptized in water?

5. Your life comes from Jesus, and the way you maintain that connection and relationship is through church. Jesus is the vine, and we are the branches. It means we have to stay connected to live. This week, go to church and make an appointment with your pastor. Get involved, and serve your pastors and church.

Chapter 18

War in the Heavenlies

We are at war. Like it or not, believe it or not, war has been declared on you. The moment you were born, you became the object of hate. You say, "Benny, whom have I offended that they have hated me since the day I was born?" The answer is simple: the devil.

You have already read about Satan and how he uses fear to intimidate and trap people into all sorts of behaviors. He was once a powerful angel who threw it all away in a bid for power. He was cast down to earth and became the enemy of everything held dear by God. He especially hates you and me because we are made in God's image. He is jealous, cunning, ruthless—and very much at work.

I know there are people who think the devil is a myth or just a cartoonish character in a red suit, holding a pitchfork. But let me tell you that he is very real and very active. And he has a large number of fallen angels who work with him to destroy you and me and anyone else who loves the Lord.

Spiritual Warfare

The idea of warfare against darkness is an old one. Some people think it is a new idea. But it is a reality that the Bible has recognized all along. The truth is that ever since Satan's rebellion in heaven, there has been war raging in the heavenlies—the spiritual realm. That war has spilled over into the physical world, and now you and I are a part of that conflict. The question is, How do we fight an enemy we cannot see? The answer is easy. It is the same way you worship God whom you cannot see—by faith. So what is spiritual warfare?

Spiritual warfare means engaging the enemy of our souls through the power of the Holy Spirit and authority of Jesus Christ operating in our lives.

It does not mean every bad thing that happens to us is caused by a demon. At times, the conflicts that come against our lives are spiritual in nature. There has been much written about spiritual warfare. But Paul said it best in Ephesians 6:10–18, where he addressed the basics of spiritual warfare for us.

Realize that we are at war and must put on our armor (vv. 10-11).

Paul told us to be strong in the Lord, which means to take courage. You are at war, but the best way to be beaten by the enemy is to deny his strength or ability. Paul said that we need to be encouraged in the Lord. Remember that the Word tells us that greater is He that is in us than he that is in the world. We must put God's armor on—otherwise we will fall for the devil's schemes. It is that simple.

Recognize that our enemy is spiritual and organized (v. 12).

Paul said that our struggle is not against flesh and blood. It is not your neighbor, boss or Osama bin Laden. Yes, we have human conflict and enemies that we have to fight at times. But ultimately our enemy—the one pulling the strings—is a hierarchy of spiritual wickedness that is organized and motivated.

God's Arsenal of Spiritual Warfare

The enemy is not going to respect the fact that you carry a Bible around. What he will respect is your faith. Putting on the armor of God indicates you have the forces of heaven behind you, and you are not on your own. Remember how David declined to wear Saul's armor when he fought Goliath? He had to do it God's way—and so do we. Besides, whose armor would you rather be wearing in a death match—God's or something you came up with? Take a closer look at God's arsenal of spiritual warfare.

1. *The belt of truth.* This represents God's Word, which must be entrenched at the center of our being. We must be anchored to the Bible because all the other weapons flow from God's truth.

2. *Breastplate of righteousness.* The heart is covered by the breastplate because the heart is the most vital organ in combat. We have to be in right standing with God. Our cause is the Lord's cause and not our own. God has declared us righteous, and we have a stake in this fight.

3. *Feet fitted with the gospel of peace.* Our testimony is another potent weapon that the enemy hates. When we tell others about Jesus or when we talk about what He has done in our lives, it builds faith in us and the person hearing our words. We also have to

protect our testimony by not doing something shameful or offensive that would make Christians look bad and hurt our witness.

4. *Shield of faith.* It is by faith that we deflect the doubts, fears and circumstances that the enemy throws our way. We must look into the unseen and not go by what we see. Sometimes things look pretty bad. The enemy says, "I told you so. You're finished!" That is when you grab your shield of faith and deflect those lies to the ground.

5. *Helmet of salvation.* We must be assured of our salvation and right standing before God. If the enemy can get into our minds and cause us to doubt that God loves us or that we really are saved, then he can take the field. Why? Once we lose confidence, our faith will begin to fail us. You must stand firm in who you are as a child of God.

6. *Sword of the Spirit.* The one offensive weapon we have is God's Word. When we speak God's Word in faith, we wield a powerful sword that cuts the enemy in pieces. He cannot stand before God's Word mixed with faith. He has to flee. (See Matthew 4:10–11.)

What Do We Do With the Weapons?

In 2 Corinthians 10, Paul writes that the weapons that we have in God are not carnal—that is flesh and blood—but they are "mighty in God for pulling down strongholds" (NKJV). If we could only get in our hearts and heads the kind of powerful weapons God has placed in our hands. If only our faith would allow us to become skilled in using those weapons. But we often act like primitive tribesmen who have stumbled upon a rifle but have no knowledge as to how it works. What does God do with the weapons? Let's read Paul's thoughts on the subject.

> For though we live in the world, we do not wage war as the world does. The weapons we fight with are not the weapons of the world. On the contrary, they have divine power to demolish strongholds. We demolish arguments and every pretension that sets itself up against the knowledge of God, and we take captive every thought to make it obedient to Christ.
>
> —2 Corinthians 10:3–5

We are not given weapons just to push devils around. There is a strategy that we become a part of when God is able to use our faith in the fight. Paul detailed the strategy of spiritual warfare for us.

We can't fight a spiritual battle with worldly methods (vv. 3–4).

It is crazy to battle a spiritual fight with worldly means. We must recognize that the enemy will respect nothing that we come up with on our own. People who think they are controlling demons through charms and incantations are only being deceived. The only real power that a demon respects is the power of God expressed through faith.

Our targets are primarily enemy strongholds (v. 4).

Strongholds are spiritual hiding grounds where there is entrenched strength, which may have been built up over the years. It can be the result of repeated sinful behavior, abuse or mental depression—anything that a demon can use to harass and influence a person. If you have ever seen a person—even a Christian—who cannot shake a particular sin or attitude—it is possible they have a stronghold operating in their lives.

Now hear me—I am not talking possession here because true Christians cannot be possessed by demons. The Holy Spirit and a fallen spirit cannot occupy the same space. But if a Christian continually falls or gives into a sin or attitude, he can open himself up to an oppressive spirit that can create a stronghold in his life. Praise God that He has given us the power to demolish strongholds.

Target prideful knowledge and counterfeit thoughts (v. 5).

In other words, God expects us to use the weapon of our wisdom to confound the arguments and confusions of the enemy. We should have a basic understanding of what we believe and why. We should be able to give a reason for our faith; we should have a working knowledge of the Scriptures. If we are not in God's Word, then we cannot effectively use this weapon called the sword of the Spirit. God's knowledge is an awesome weapon, but we have to get it in our brains first. That means reading and memorizing the Bible.

We also target our own imagination (v. 5).

The mind is a great battlefield. If we cannot control our lustful imaginations or angry thoughts, how can we ever expect to be effective? If the battlefield is the mind, and our mind is messed up, it does not take a Ph.D. to figure out that we are not going to fight very well. We have to be responsible for our thoughts. We have to be careful of what we allow in our minds through what we read, watch and do.

We Win in the End

The great news is this: Satan and his army have already been defeated! They were taken out at the Resurrection. The Bible says the devil and his angels have been disarmed and beaten. (See Colossians 2:15.) So we do not have to be afraid. While he can harass and attack us, Satan can only go as far as we allow him to go.

We still have to wage a relentless war. Peter said we should remain alert. (See 1 Peter 5:8.) We have to fight in God's strength on all levels of the mind and emotions. We have to keep our arsenal pure through obedience to God and filled with His Word so that our faith remains active and alive. Our weapons are unsurpassed in their ability to deal with the enemy. Let's use them to God's glory!

TURNING UPSIDE DOWN

1. After reading this chapter, can you recognize a situation in your life that is not a physical struggle but a spiritual battle?

2. How can you change your reaction to this situation now that you recognize it as spiritual?

Chapter 19

A Person of Passion

Charles Spurgeon once wrote, "No heart of a child of God will ever be satisfied with any object or person short of the Lord Jesus Christ."[1] And in his memoirs, Charles Finney, one of the great evangelists of the last century, described his determination to obtain the passion of God in his life. God had been dealing with him, and he decided that it was time either to accept God or "die in the attempt." He found his way to a clearing in the woods near his law office in Adams, New York, a place where the trees formed a natural altar. He began to pray. Finney wrestled in prayer as he recounted past sins and failures in his life. The hours went by until "all sense of sin, all consciousness of present sin or guilt had departed from me." Peace had finally come to Charles Finney.

Finney returned to the law office. It was now dusk, and everyone had departed for the day. But the Holy Spirit was not finished yet, as Finney was drawn to a back room to continue in prayer. Read Finney's account of his wonderful experience:

> There was no light in the room; nevertheless, it appeared to me as it were perfectly light. As I went in

and shut the door it seemed as if I met the Lord Jesus face to face—as I would see any other man. He said nothing, but looked at me in such a manner as to break me right down at His feet. It seemed to me a reality that He stood before me, and I fell down at His feet and poured my soul out to Him. I wept like a child and bathed His feet with my tears.[2]

After the encounter with Jesus, Finney went into the next room and sat by the fire, thinking on the vision of Christ, when he recalled:

> …I received a mighty baptism by the Holy Ghost. Without expecting it, the Holy Spirit descended upon me in a manner that seemed to go through my body and soul. I could feel the impression like a wave of electricity going through me. Indeed it seemed to come in waves and waves of liquid love…like the very breath of God…These waves came over me and over me until I recollect I cried out, "I shall die if these waves continue to pass over me…Lord, I cannot bear anymore."[3]

You can understand why Finney's life was never the same after this tremendous encounter with Jesus. He eventually gave up his law career to become a preacher. His revivals in upstate New York became world famous. Finney had a passion for God that was unquenchable, and it stemmed from a personal encounter with Jesus.

God Seeks People of Passion

God is looking for people of passion who are willing to find an altar in the woods, in their homes or wherever they can be alone with God.

God is looking for people who hunger and thirst after righteousness and will not be satisfied until they have been filled—people who desire God more than anything else.

What is passion? It is an intensely emotional or compelling attitude, a feeling that calls people to action. It is a strong affection or love, great enthusiasm or desire, or a violent anger. Passion evokes images of ardor, zeal and fervor. When James said that the "effective prayer of a righteous man can accomplish much," he spoke of a fervent passion to pray (James 5:16, NAS).

Passionate, Not Passive

We should pursue passionate, not passive Christianity. God has enough passive Christians to revive. Passionate Christians are the ones who will accomplish great things for the kingdom.

To be passive means one is:

- Enduring or submitting without resistance.
- Inactive; not reacting visibly.
- Being acted upon rather than acting upon.

Being passive is not necessarily a bad thing. Our attitude *toward* God must be passive—we submit to God without resistance and allow Him to act upon us. But our attitude *for* God must be passionate. By being passionate, we can take on the gates of hell as God leads us from victory to victory.

Passionate People Are Powerful People

History shows us that men and women of passion—for good or evil—have moved nations. In the right setting, passion can be a glorious motivator for positive change, such as Abraham Lincoln's attempts to end slavery and hold the Union together at all costs. In the wrong setting, however, passion can lead to disaster. Have you ever seen the old newsreels of Adolf Hitler? The man might have been a monster, but he used the art of passion to inflame a crowd, make them his willing subjects and plunge the world into war.

Passion for God Is a Relational Experience, Not Just Emotional

Passion is an ever-present reality based upon our knowing Jesus. If passion were simply an emotional reaction to God, there would be downtimes when our passion would fizzle out. But we know that we can be completely drained of physical strength yet still have a passion for God based upon the truth of our relationship with Him. Passion is maintained by faith, not feelings. The passion of God delivered to us by the Holy Spirit can give us the ability to accomplish tremendous things.

Paul addressed this when he wrote:

> For what man knows the things of a man except the spirit of the man which is in him? Even so no one knows the things of God except the Spirit of God. Now we have received, not the spirit of the world, but the Spirit who is from God, that we might know the things that have been freely given to us by God. These things we also speak, not in words which man's wisdom teaches but which the Holy Spirit teaches, comparing spiritual things with spiritual.
>
> —1 CORINTHIANS 2:11–13, NKJV

It is the Holy Spirit who knows the mind of God intimately enough to forward His will to us. The Spirit must lead us into passionate relationship with the Father so we can understand

His spiritual truths and activate them here on earth.

The Bible is rich with the stories of men and women who developed a passion for God, which led them to do tremendous exploits.

- Joseph's passion for God enabled him to overcome the temptations of Potiphar's wife and be cast in prison rather than compromise.

- Daniel's passion for God led him to defy the king's decrees not to pray, even at the risk of his life.

- Stephen's passion for God gave him the courage to testify about the Lord to the Sanhedrin before he was dragged out and stoned.

Let's take a look at another person of passion and how he turned his world upside down: King Saul. His story is found in the Book of 1 Samuel. Taken as a whole, the life of Saul is a tragic picture of the results of disobedience to God. There are some wonderful moments, however, in the life of Saul, which illustrate the importance as well as the result of having passion for God. The road to kingship for Saul began rather ignobly. Saul was searching for his father's lost donkeys when he came to the town where the prophet Samuel was ministering. Saul decided that Samuel might be able to tell him where the animals were. In the meantime, the Lord had instructed Samuel to anoint this stranger as king. Reluctantly, Saul accepted the kingship, although they had to dig him out of the baggage where he was hiding. (See 1 Samuel 10:20–23.)

Saul was certainly unproven, and he had little self-confidence. He was not even a good hider. Fortunately, God has a way of putting us in situations requiring passion on our part so we can see Him move, and this is exactly what happened to

Saul. God stirred up a cause worth fighting for in Saul. Let's pick up the text in 1 Samuel 11 and watch a passive man evolve into a man of passion:

> Then Nahash the Ammonite came up and encamped against Jabesh Gilead; and all the men of Jabesh said to Nahash, "Make a covenant with us, and we will serve you." And Nahash the Ammonite answered them, "On this condition I will make a covenant with you, that I may put out all your right eyes, and bring reproach on all Israel." Then the elders of Jabesh said to him, "Hold off for seven days, that we may send messengers to all the territory of Israel. And then, if there is no one to save us, we will come out to you."
>
> —1 Samuel 11:1–3, NKJV

Bullies have always been around, it seems, even in biblical times. A local ruler of the Ammonites decided to inflict himself upon the people of Jabesh Gilead, a little town near the Jordan River. The Ammonites were distant cousins of the Israelites (the result of an incestuous episode between Lot and his youngest daughter in Genesis 19). They were notorious hit-and-run fighters with little stomach for real war.

Nahash, the Ammonite leader, is a type of Satan; his name means "serpent." Like Satan, Nahash was brash, proud and willing to settle, as long as it was to his advantage. He was quite confident of his position, or he would not have been making such bold demands. He especially would not have allowed the elders the seven days grace they requested unless he felt sure of his position. He was bent on humiliating the people of God as well as taking spoils. The mutilation of the population would bring a reproach on the nation for their inability to rescue one of their own cities, signaling not only the defeat of Israel but also of God. A passive population that had no stomach for a fight and could not depend upon relief from elsewhere inhabited the city of Jabesh Gilead. So they decided that it was better to settle with the enemy than be destroyed by him.

Jabesh Gilead means "a dry place," an appropriate name for a city whose people were spiritually dry and passive. When we become dried out and passive in our Christian walk, we are the most vulnerable to an attack by the enemy. It is in this instance that we would rather make a treaty with the enemy than fight him. This is exactly the place where the people of Jabesh Gilead found themselves.

Dealing With the Enemy

The people of God approached the enemy about making a covenant first. Of course, the devil is willing to make a deal, especially with God's people. Remember that although he is powerful, Satan only has limited resources. It costs him less to settle than to fight, so why not settle? In the case of Judas Iscariot, it cost him only thirty pieces of silver. Charles H. Spurgeon, one of the great preachers of the last century, said the following concerning the devil in one of his sermons:

> He is more cunning than the wisest: How soon he entangled Solomon! He is stronger than the strongest: How fatally he overthrew Samson! Yes, and men after God's own heart, like David, have been led into most grievous sins by his seductions.[4]

To enter into covenant with Satan is to place yourself under house arrest; you have freedom to move about, but you are imprisoned all the same.

When we become dry or passive in our relationship with

God, we will begin to settle with the enemy, making deals and compromising our integrity until we are in servitude to him.

We find ourselves saying things like:

- "It's not so bad."
- "God will understand."
- "Nobody's perfect."
- "It's just a little thing!"
- "It's OK. God will forgive me."

To enter into a deal with darkness is to buy into a lie. Once ground is given, it becomes a narcotic to the enemy—he is never satisfied and will continue asking for more and more until he has everything. Believe me, Satan is a master of the old "you-didn't-read-the-fine-print" ploy. That fine print has cost people their families, jobs and even their lives. The people of Jabesh Gilead did not realize with whom they were dealing.

Let's Make a Deal

Just as we can only deal with the Lord on His terms, Satan will only come to terms with us if it is according to his plan. Nahash accepted the offer of a settlement and immediately set the conditions of the covenant. If Satan senses that we are willing to settle, he knows he has the advantage already and will begin upping the ante accordingly. The demand in Nahash's case was the gouging out of everyone's right eye. There are a couple of reasons for this unusual stipulation:

- *Disgrace would be brought on God's people because they were unable to prevent this from happening.* Satan does not want just to win; he wants the humiliation of everything that stands for God. When he disgraces the people of God, he brings reproach on the church and on God's credibility in the eyes of the world. Just think back to the black eye Christians took in the late 1980s during the televangelists' scandals.

- *Disabling the people takes the fight out of them for future conflicts.* Because most men held a shield in their left hand and a sword in their right when they fought, the losing of their right eye would render them useless in a war. They could not see to fight. When the warrior would lift up his shield to defend against the enemy, the only eye he could see out of was his right eye.

So to gouge out the right eye would make a warrior powerless to strike back in an offensive manner. Therefore, there would be an army dressed up in all of their armor but unable to inflict any damage to the enemy. The enemy wants to take the fight out of Christians by disabling us so that we will not be interested in a rematch. He will attack us physically, emotionally, spiritually—however he can—until we become passive and ultimately tamed.

A Cry for Help

The elders appealed to Nahash for seven days to seek help. These men could still remember the valiant men of old who did not compromise with the enemy. These elders had enough wisdom to ask for seven days (God's number of completion) to seek help. Nahash agreed to this, knowing that there was little, if any, chance that help would come in seven days. We must be alert to signals that passive people send out. Just because people have become passive, even to the point of numbness, does not mean that the Spirit of God cannot rekindle life in them. As God seeks to deliver people from their passive prisons and turn their world upside down, we must be the instruments to help and encourage them.

How Can You Tell When Someone Is in a Passive Prison?

There are some indicators for passive people:

- They do not worship.
- They neglect God's Word.
- They are not careful about what they read or watch.
- They do not attend church.
- They are silent in their witness.

In 1 Samuel 11:4, the Bible says messengers were sent out across Israel to appeal for help. Who do you suppose they selected for the mission, men of passivity or passion?

I can guarantee that at a time like this, men of passion were needed to carry the urgency of the message as to what was at stake.

I believe these were men who were probably married with many children. They likely had the vision of their wives and children seeing their right eyes gouged out. This would spur these men to get help because there was something at stake back in their city. There was a cause to be passionate about, and nothing was going to quench their passion to get help. These were men in Jabesh Gilead who had not succumbed to the dryness of life. These handpicked men of passion were on a mission to save their friends and loved ones. And so are we.

> So the messengers came to Gibeah of Saul and told the news in the hearing of the people. And all the people lifted up their voices and wept. Now there was Saul, coming behind the herd from the field; and Saul said, "What troubles the people, that they weep?" And they told him the words of the men of Jabesh.
>
> —1 Samuel 11:4–5, NKJV

The message of the plight of their fellow Jews caused the people to weep in compassion. Today, I look at what is happening to the United States. I see the passivity and compromise as the enemy has dealt severely with us. America has departed from our God, and it makes me weep. Anyone who loves this country can see the troubles we are in. Yet, we must move beyond an emotional response and get down to hard-core action if we are going to see our globe impacted and this country God-centered once again.

If there is one thing that stirs Americans to unified action, it is the belief in a cause. It is a part of the American spirit woven into the fabric of our nation from the very beginning. Christians must see the spiritual renewal of America as a cause worth fighting for, just as Saul saw a cause in the Jabesh situation.

> Then the Spirit of God came upon Saul when he heard this news, and his anger was greatly aroused.
> —1 SAMUEL 11:6, NKJV

When Saul heard what the messengers had to say, he was furious. Suddenly, the responsibilities of being king took on a new meaning. There was a cause that was worthy of a fight. The Spirit of God came upon Saul as he got mad at the devil. The enemy always looks smaller in the eyes of faith and passion.

A passion was created in Saul by the Holy Spirit, who built his faith and set him on a course of action.

Passion Produces Action

> So he took a yoke of oxen and cut them in pieces, and sent them throughout all the territory of Israel by the hands of messengers, saying, "Whoever does not go out with Saul and Samuel to battle, so it shall be done to his

oxen." And the fear of the LORD fell on the people, and they came out with one consent. When he numbered them in Bezek, the children of Israel were three hundred thousand, and the men of Judah thirty thousand.

—1 SAMUEL 11:7–8, NKJV

A call to arms went throughout the different tribes by way of a rather gruesome message: pieces of Saul's oxen. The point is clear—all of us are affected by the enemy, so we must all fight or pay a heavy price. Paul's comparison of the body of Christ to the human body and all the parts needing to work together is a similar situation. (See Romans 12:4–13.) When one part of the body hurts, it affects the whole. Saul was telling the people that if they did not come and help fight the battle, eventually the fight would come to them, and nobody would help them.

Give, and it shall be given unto you. Help someone else, and you will be given help when you need it.

This was also a critical test of Saul's new role as king. He was about to find out if his passion could move a nation to war. The results affirmed his leadership, as well as the Lord's active participation on behalf of Saul. The fear of the Lord came upon them and helped convince them to fight.

The Enemy Scattered

Saul sent word to the elders at Jabesh that he would bring deliverance to them within a day. The people were elated as they told the Ammonites that they would surrender the next day and succumb to whatever they had in mind.

Let's see what happened when Saul's army attacked:

So it was, on the next day, that Saul put the people in three companies; and they came into the midst of the camp in the morning watch, and killed Ammonites until the heat of the day. And it happened that those who survived were scattered, so that no two of them were left together.

—1 SAMUEL 11:11, NKJV

Nahash got more than he bargained for. He was anticipating a cheap victory, but he became passive. It cost him the battle. The enemy does not stand a chance against a people who are passionate for God. We must realize that the Lord calls us to do battle with the devil so we can release from captivity those who have been ensnared by him. God also wants us to scatter the enemy and drive him out of the land. This can only be done through a passionate people with a passionate cause empowered by the Holy Spirit.

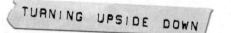

TURNING UPSIDE DOWN

1. After reading this chapter, do you see yourself as a passionate or passive person?

2. The Holy Spirit is the one who gives passionate Christians the ability to accomplish the Lord's will. What is God calling you to do? What action needs to take place?

3. How do you regain the passion that you had before? Our passion for God is based upon our relationship with Him and spending time with Him. Is the Holy Spirit calling you to spend more quality time in His presence? What can you rearrange to accommodate extra time with Him?

Chapter 20

When the Attack Comes

As you seek to turn the world upside down for Jesus, a time will come when the world will turn on you. That is because darkness resists light and does anything it can to keep from being exposed for what it is. There are young people all over the world who are in bondage to sex, drugs, abusive relationships—and on their way to hell—unless somebody is willing to step in and rescue them—even if it means a fight.

The apostles Peter and John were willing to step out, shortly after Jesus ascended to heaven. Read the account in Acts 4:1–31.

Look at the circumstances. God used Peter and John to do a great miracle, but they were persecuted and told to be quiet about their faith. Their faith and desire for revival were attacked. What can we learn from their situation and reaction?

Religion Is Always Suspicious of Legitimate Faith

The religious people targeted Peter and John. They went to church and had the program down, but they lacked God's power and presence. There are religious people today who do the same thing. They may come to you and say, "By what power are you doing this? You are acting like extraordinary Christians; you shouldn't be this way." They try to verbally attack you. But look at Peter's response in Acts 4:10. He said their power came "by the name of Jesus Christ." In Acts 4:12, Peter said Jesus is the only way.

The Religious People Knew Peter and John Were With Jesus

People like to hang around the real thing—even if they do not understand it. The problem with religious people is they become suspicious and jealous. They do not understand that the same power is available to them as well.

They knew that Peter and John had been with Jesus because it showed. There was something unique about them—they had been with Jesus. When you walk into a smoke-filled room, you smell like smoke. When you are immersed in the presence of God, His Word, will and ways permeate your life. Some of you are so fired up and in love with Jesus, you are burning in your soul as you read the Word and pray. God's presence is evident in you.

If you are frozen in fear, you can never step out in faith and do what God has called you to do. The religious people threatened and intimidated Peter and John, which are common ploys of the devil. He says, "If I just kind of talk big to them, they'll back down." So they commanded the two apostles not to speak at all in the name of Jesus.

Peter and John Responded in Faith

The duo's first action was prayer, which is our lifeline to Almighty God. In Acts 4:23, they went to their fellow disciples. Peter and John knew that they needed people who were holding on to faith to help them at their point of need. This is the key: You cannot do it alone. Sometimes you fall and cannot get up.

That is why you need somebody with you. When you are under attack, they will say, "You know what, you are going to make it. Let me give you some confidence, courage, assurance and effective strategy." You must surround yourself with believers who will encourage your faith. You need to get with like-minded Christians when you are under attack. The Bible says, "Two are better than one…If one falls down, his friend can help him up. But pity the man who falls and has no one to help him up!" (Eccles. 4:9–10). You need someone to help you turn your world upside down.

Peter and John Reported the Things That Were Said to Them

They did not just keep it to themselves or try to figure it out on their own. They poured out their heart regarding the threats by the religious people. I am not telling you to be phony or to deny what is going on in your life. I am telling you to get with some Christian friends and pour your heart out to them. However, you do not need to sit there and cry on each other's shoulders, saying, "It's going to get better; let's talk about it." We need more than just support; we need to get victory.

Notice what the disciples did? In Acts 4:24–30, they went to prayer. Prayer is our connection to the Almighty. Prayer will change your life because prayer changes things.

They raised their voices to God with one accord.

Their first prayer action was to cry out to God as everyone joined in. What is the key point? There is power in unity. The Bible says that one will chase a thousand, but two will chase ten thousand. (See Deuteronomy 32:30.) Raise your voice to God in passionate prayer.

They declared the power of God.

They said, "God, You are Lord of heaven and earth, and You created everything." When it comes to your prayer life, you need to forget about your problems for a while and declare the greatness of God. Do you know what will happen? Your faith will increase because you will realize that you are praying to a really big God.

Some of you, however, dive right into your problems when you pray, which magnifies your troubles. Instead, you must magnify God, who is bigger than any problem. You have to magnify God to understand that your problem is not as big as He is. Before the disciples asked for anything, they affirmed the greatness of God. They put the greatness of God in their minds and spirits.

They declared the problem that they were facing.

They told the Lord what they were facing: "God, look at their threats. God, look at this." God already knew about the threats, but the disciples were confident that they would see the answer because they prayed focused prayers. We must pray focused prayers if we are going to turn our world upside down.

They presented specific requests.

In Philippians 4:6, the Bible says, "Let your requests be made known to God" (NKJV). They were definite and specific in the things that they asked for.

They prayed, "Let us speak Your Word with boldness." They did not pray, "O Lord, help us find a safe shelter now because everybody is against us. O God, take the problems away." They said, "God, it is getting tough out there, so make me tougher in here." Every day before you go to school or work, you need to say, "Lord, enable me to speak the Word with boldness. I am not going to step back; I am going forward with You, God."

What Is Boldness?

Boldness is freedom of speech; it is the opposite of fear and cowardice. It is being outspoken and standing with a backbone even when everything is coming against you. It is saying, "He alone is my rock and my salvation; he is my fortress, and I will never be shaken" (Ps. 62:2). That is boldness. What is the key point? Prayer is the power that keeps us from backing down. Prayer keeps us plugged into the power source.

Here are some examples of bold people in the Bible:

- *Elijah on Mount Carmel.* He was outnumbered eight hundred fifty to one. He did not say, "O God, please take me away from this." He boldly stood up and said, "God, I pray right now that You will send fire down."

- *David.* He had boldness when he faced Goliath. He ran toward the giant—not away from him.

- *Daniel.* The Bible says that they made an edict in his country that banned praying to any other god except to the king. Before this became law, do you know what

Daniel used to do? He prayed three times a day on his knees with the windows wide open for all to see. Daniel did not stop praying, so they threw him in the lions' den. Daniel said, *"My God is in control."* Some of you would not have lasted long in the lions' den because you have not fostered a life of faith and revival. *You will not make it in the den of lions unless you can make it on the outside.*

You must have boldness to combat the enemy's threats, but it only comes through prayer.

For their last requests, the disciples asked for healings and signs and wonders to be done through the mighty name of Jesus. Our message must be accompanied by the power of God. Backed by prayer and His power, we can accomplish the impossible.

God's Awesome Response

After they prayed, the place was shaken. (See Acts 4:31.) God needs to shake some things off of us. When we get serious with prayer, He shakes off our complacency, comfort zones and compromising ways, which keep us in the bondage of the enemy.

The disciples were then filled with the Holy Spirit. Ephesians 5:18 says we need to be filled with the Holy Spirit always. The disciples then spoke the Word with boldness. Prayer will help you hold on to the life of faith and revival. If the early church needed to pray, how much more do we need to do the same thing?

When the Attack Comes

TURNING UPSIDE DOWN

1. Fear is the greatest enemy of faith. Identify some of your fears. Take some time and find scriptures that counteract those fears—for example, rejection versus nothing separating us from the love of God. (See Romans 8:39).

2. Do these fears hinder your boldness for Jesus? What would be the worst possible outcome if you stepped out and witnessed in order to overcome your fear? For example, would you be embarrassed?

3. Is this outcome worth your friends coming to Christ? If you knew that your boldness would plant a seed in the heart of your friend who might come to Christ, would it be worth being embarrassed?

4. Then shake it off or change your focus. As your spiritual coach, I am telling you to shake off that fear and refocus on the game of life. Life or death is at stake. There should be no fear that holds you back from winning people to the Lord and living a victorious, joyful life.

Chapter 21

What's Church Got to Do With It?

What do you think of when you hear the word *fellowship*? Do you think of home groups, potlucks or maybe a church picnic? Yes, fellowship often happens around a meal, but I want to talk about fellowship in terms of life centered around Christ.

In 1 Corinthians 14:1, Paul said we are to follow the "way of love." He said this is a hallmark of true Christianity. The supreme example of the way of love is Jesus Himself. Jesus told His disciples that we are to love each other as He loved us. (See John 13:34.) So, to follow the way of Christ is to follow the way of love, laying down your life for a friend.

Christian fellowship is one of the greatest examples of love. It allows us to encourage, build up, pray for and find meaningful relationships with one another. I know some of you cannot wait to be married. That is OK. I waited thirty-three years for the right person, and let me tell you, it was well worth it. But here is a piece of advice for you: The person you marry had better be someone with whom you are able to have pure Christian fellowship before marriage. What do I mean?

The Family of God

We have been adopted into the greatest family ever created—the family of God. That is right. If you are a Christian, then we are family. Yeah, I know some families are really weird. That is OK. Some Christians are really weird, but we are still family. The place where we practice being family most of all is at church.

Now I know some of you did not like church when you were young because it was boring, or maybe you go to a church right now that is boring. Pray about finding an exciting church. Find a youth group that is connected to the power of God. Find a church that knows how to worship and a place where God's power is made real in the services. It is important for you to get into a church.

I have heard many complain, "Benny, the church my parents go to is full of old people." So start blessing the older people. Another complaint: "Benny, I don't like the music at my church." So start learning how to worship God in other ways. Worship is not all about the music. Worship is your attitude before the Lord. Someday you will be old enough to make a decision about church. Until that day comes, you need to honor your parents and go to their church. Perhaps you have a friend whose church has a passionate youth group; ask your parents if you can attend that congregation. The point is to be in fellowship at church. (See Hebrews 10:25.)

What Does Church Do?

Church is a word that means "gathering" or "assembly." It is a place where Christians come to celebrate their redemption in the Lord. Church is also a place where the lost can find salvation. It is a place of worship, fellowship and healing. In short, church is a place for life. Church is your lifeline to a healthy relationship with God. Why? God made you to be in relationship with other believers. That is why it is called the BODY of Christ—not the toenail of Christ.

Four Functions of Church

If you have ever looked in a phone book under "churches," you have probably seen a lot of listings. That is because not every church is the same. Some are big, and some are small. Some are Catholic, and some are Protestant. Some are Pentecostal, while others are Baptist. Some are part of a denomination, and some are independent. If they are Bible-believing churches who love the Lord, then there are four basics that they should be involved in regarding their mission to the world.

1. Evangelism

The primary goal of any church—the very reason Christ created the church—is to evangelize the world. A church should exist to build the kingdom by increasing the number of saved people. Churches that are healthy obey the Great Commission, making them soul-winning congregations.

Think about your church. When was the last time someone became born again? Consider your youth congregation—have you seen young people won to Jesus lately? Have you ever brought your non-Christian friends to church with you? I am telling you that young people are on their way to hell. Unless you start turning their world upside down, they will never make it to heaven. Jesus said we should pray for laborers to go into the harvest fields and work them. (See Matthew 9:38.)

When was the last time you led someone to the Lord? When was the last time you tried? We need to get out of our comfortable youth groups and get to our city streets and school campuses so we can shake the world for Jesus. God's church should be filled up, but it will not happen unless we are out there telling people about Jesus and getting them into church. (See Luke 14:23.)

2. Connection

After people become Christians, they need a healthy place to grow and hang out. The church is a place where people can make friends with other Christians and grow in the Lord. Think of how you felt the first day you came into your youth group. Did you feel alone? Did someone reach out to you?

That is what church can provide for people who have been disconnected from the Lord. People want to be connected, and church is the best place to get plugged into the body of Christ. What am I saying? Start approaching guests at your church, and make them feel wanted and special. Reach out beyond your own circle of friends, and build the body of Christ from the inside out—one life at a time.

3. Discipleship

Once people are connected to the Lord and start coming to church, there is another important step that must happen. Church provides a place where people can begin to grow in their faith. You did not just begin maturing overnight. It was a process that began as you were discipled.

One of the functions of the church is to disciple. This means taking people from wherever they are in their walk with Jesus and helping them in their growth, knowledge and experience of God. Does your church have a discipleship program in place? If not, why don't you begin by meeting with a new believer on a regular basis? Discipleship must happen in a church, or it is not a Great Commission congregation.

4. Involvement

Another important part of our walk with Jesus that a church provides is an opportunity to become involved in ministry. For some, it might mean joining the worship band or praise team. For others, it might mean teaching a class or helping out in the children's department.

When Christians get involved in the church:

- They discover and use their spiritual gifts.
- They bless others with their ministry.

The church provides a place where people can practice their faith and help build the kingdom of God. Everyone likes to be useful, which is part of God's design and desire for us. By becoming involved in the work of the church, we grow more like Jesus, giving of ourselves and building the body of Christ.

Your Call to Destiny

Ultimately, the church helps us have a sense of destiny and purpose. Pastors are a gift to the church because they help equip the people for works of service. (See Ephesians 4:11–12.) By fulfilling a ministry in the church, a person develops a sense of calling and purpose. God has a destiny for all of us. It makes sense that He would flesh it out among His people.

The church gives us a reason for being. Jesus gave us the church so that it may become a place where His gifts can be used and where our love for each other can be expressed.

The church is essentially the boat on which we navigate the waters of life. A lot of people try to switch boats to get through a storm or challenge, not understanding that we are all in the same water. That is why it is important to find a church where you truly fit and stick it out. Storms come, and emotions rage; some people will not make it through every storm, but just hold on. Stay where the Lord told you to go. If you want to leave your church, DO NOT leave until He says so.

We have talked about it in a previous chapter—the idea of simply replacing anything in our lives that we feel does not work anymore. Instead of walking out the tough situations, we simply avoid, ignore or run away from them. The body of Christ is a family. Unfortunately, it is made up of fallible beings like you and me. We make mistakes, so just like in a natural family, you will get offended and hurt. But getting offended does not justify leaving. We are not talking about gross sin here. We are talking about little offenses and petty conflicts—the little foxes that the Bible says spoil the vineyard. (See Song of Solomon 2:15.) We would not want our natural family to be torn apart because of attitude problems. In the same manner, God does not want His family to be torn apart because of these issues. Stay where you are planted. You will not always like it, and it will not always be what you want. But if God said you are supposed to be there, then it is where you will prosper and grow.

TURNING UPSIDE DOWN

1. Think about the kind of church you would like to go to. Do you know how to change your church? You start by being the kind of person you want in a church and influence others.

2. Are you completely committed to church?

3. Do you have unresolved conflict from a past church? You know bitterness only affects you. That pastor or church has gone on, and you are the one bound up in unforgiveness. Take some time right now and release that hurt or offense. It is not worth a lifetime without fellowship and godly wisdom.

Chapter 22

The Ultimate Upside-Down Experience: Revival

As we get near the end of this section, I want to take a look at revival. We will take a look at Jesus' entrance into Jerusalem during the last week of His life and how revival came to that great city. (See Matthew 21:1–17.) Some people knew it—others missed it completely. And yet they all saw the King.

Jesus' Triumphal Entry

When Jesus came into the city, He did not stop for the multitudes, but He went straight to the temple of God—the church at the time. The focus of Jesus was the church. What does that mean?

God is visiting our nation and the world right now, but He is not visiting America so much in the streets. He is visiting us in the churches again.

Jesus is on a mission today to get His church back in the right order. What good would it do if God suddenly touched everyone out there that needs Him, and they ran to dead churches? We are dealing with a whole generation of young people who do not want church because their parents had bad church experiences, or they went to morgue like congregations instead of lively churches. That is why God is stirring up revival. I know some of you are going to get upset at me and say, "How dare you say that about our church?" But why has society gotten worse instead of better? Why has church attendance decreased in America in the last five years?

Or maybe you say, "I am in a church, isn't that good enough, preacher?" NO. Just because you camped out in your garage week in and week out, it does not make you a car. Just because you come to church week in and week out, it does not mean you are right with God. Your heart will tell you if you are right with God.

The Holy Spirit will bring conviction to your heart and mine, saying, "This has to get right because this is going to kill you, and I have a better plan for your life." Jesus wants His anointing to be on us. Why do we need this anointing?

Why do we need His presence? He needs us to be Jesus to the world.

Steps to Turn Your World Upside Down Through Revival

There are four steps to turn your world upside down through revival.

1. Purity is a requirement.

God wants to bring purity to the body of Christ. In Matthew 21:12, the Bible says Jesus drove out the ones that were using the church for personal gain. He kicked out those that bought and sold in the temple. He overturned the tables of the money changers. Jesus was not afraid to confront people in love. He was purifying His church. What is God looking for first and foremost? He is looking for purity in the church again.

I know that this is not a popular message. Our culture says, "If it feels good, then do it. There's no absolute truth." You may say, "But I want to do my own thing." Your own thing is really a demonically inspired deception. You are really doing the devil's thing, and it leads to death. You can drive on the other side of the road because you feel like doing it, but sooner or later, you will kill yourself and probably others as well. Whether this world believes it or not, there is truth—absolute truth.

Jesus said, "I am the way, the truth, and the life. No one comes to the Father except through Me" (John 14:6, NKJV). There are not many roads leading to the same place. If that is the case, then Jesus died in vain.

Purity is very important to God:

- In 2 Timothy 2:20–21, the Bible says there are many vessels in the house of God, but if you purify yourself you will be a vessel for honorable use. Do you want to be used honorably in the kingdom of God? God is looking for purity.

- Matthew 5:8 says the pure in heart shall see God. This means the impure will not see God. How do you get pure again? Allow the blood of Jesus Christ to wash and make you new again through the forgiveness of sin.

- In 1 John l:9, the scripture says purity comes through the blood of Jesus. "If we confess our sins, He is faithful and just to forgive us our sins and to cleanse us from all unrighteousness" (NKJV).

2. A house of prayer is the result of purity.

Do you know why it is sometimes hard to pray? It is because

of the impurity in our hearts. God wants to deal with the heart. When you have really blown it and do not confess and repent, it is hard for you to pray. Deal with the purity of your heart first. Purity will lead to prayer.

Do you know what causes revival? Why is God moving in so many ways and in so many places? Why is He blessing the ministry I am involved with right now? Why is His hand on the church we started in Las Vegas? The answer to all these questions is *prayer*.

Jesus said men ought always to pray and never give up. (See Luke 18:1.) Do you have any lost loved ones? Pray and do not give up. Do you have some lost kids? Pray and do not give up. Are things going bad in your life? Pray and do not give up. You have to keep praying. Why? Keep praying because He is listening, and if He is listening, He will answer you.

When I was a youth pastor in Marysville, Washington, we went on a three-year prayer and fasting vigil for our youth church. Some people never missed a Friday night for prayer. People often asked how it happened. God moved on the hearts of young people to pray for their lost friends and to see the power of God fall in our services. That is how revival happened.

Jesus said, "My house will be called a house of prayer" (Matt. 21:13). What is the beginning of revival in our world?

> If my people, which are called by my name, shall humble themselves, and pray, and seek my face, and turn from their wicked ways; then will I hear from heaven, and will forgive their sin, and will heal their land.
>
> —2 Chronicles 7:14, KJV

Do you want to see the Lord move in your country? Then Christians have to start getting it right with the Lord through confession and repentance. Only THEN will He turn and heal our land.

3. Purity plus prayer equals power.

In Matthew 21:14, after the temple was purified for prayer, the power of God came as the blind and lame got healed.

I want God to do similar great miracles, authenticated by doctors, so that it will shock the world, convincing them that God is alive. The church needs to be a house of power again. We have been powerless in the church for too long. It is about time people walk in and say, "Man, there is power in that place."

When prodigals come back, the church must be a house of purity and prayer, but also a house of power. God is the source of our power, enabling and equipping us in our struggle with the enemy. Nothing compares to the power of God. It is the power that raised Christ from the dead. His power defeated Satan at the cross and enabled the apostles to turn the world upside down, which was recorded in the Book of Acts. The same power is quickening us today. The power is present to heal, save, set free and answer the lies, destruction and manipulation of the devil. The power of God resides in vessels that are purified, prayerful and willing to be used in unusual ways. It is not for the fainthearted or easily frightened; the power is real and amazing. It is the connection of an infinite being to a finite man. God's power will rock your world, mind and body. You must believe in its power.

I have been asked many times, "Why do people fall when you pray for them?" Or, "Why do people cry uncontrollably when you pray?" First, I do not know, and second, I just believe. When I pray for someone, I believe they will really feel God beyond head knowledge and experience His power in their life.

Why are our televisions filled with reality shows? It is

because this generation longs to know the reality of God. They are bored with fantasy; they want reality. They are bored with games; they want worship. They are bored with contests; they want the Word. This generation wants God and wants it raw. They need to know that He is real and more powerful than the drugs they take, the incantations they recite or the rave last weekend. God is real, and He is relevant.

God's power is present today. It is happening in the Third World. In Argentina, maimed and shriveled-up arms and legs are growing during church services. That is why Argentina is experiencing the greatest revival in the world currently. And it is not just in Argentina; all over the world God is moving.

Miraculous healings are taking place. Do you know what my prayer is now for our church? "Lord, You have made us a house of prayer; turn us into a house of power. I want people who have problems with demons and are messed up on drugs and alcohol to walk into this place. As they come to be prayed for, these things start leaping out of them so that they are totally set free by the power of God." We need to become the house of power.

> My speech and my preaching were not with persuasive words of human wisdom, but in demonstration of the Spirit and of power.
> —1 Corinthians 2:4, NKJV

> For the kingdom of God is not in word but in power.
> —1 Corinthians 4:20, NKJV

But it is only a house of power if we make it a house of prayer, and it is only a house of prayer if we say, "God, cleanse us and make us a house of purity."

4. Purity, prayer and power lead us to praise.

What is the last thing that happened during Jesus' triumphal entry? In Matthew 21:15, the Bible says the people suddenly shouted awesome and deafening praise. We need to get praise back into the church. We must get excited again and bring the shout back into the church.

If there is purity, then there will be prayer, which then releases God's power. And we will be unable to hold back the praise as we see those in bondage set free, the sick healed and the lame made whole. There is nothing quite like seeing someone who has been set free praising the Lord. Nothing can match the praise of someone who has been forgiven, healed and made whole.

TURNING UPSIDE DOWN

1. Where are you in your life of purity? What areas do you need to address? Make a list of specific areas that you need to target. Pray for those areas daily, and give them to God.

2. Do you participate in corporate prayer times?

3. Have you experienced the power of God personally?

4. The Bible says to desire spiritual gifts. (See 1 Corinthians 14:1.) Ask the Lord to release His power in a new way to you. Ask Him specifically to let you experience His power.

Upside-Down Destiny

You have just read some insights I have learned that are a beginning point for a life of faith. Your destiny and success in turning your world upside down must be birthed from your heart. You must believe it is your destiny for God to use you to impact your generation. I call this generation...

The Josiah Generation

In case you have not noticed, we live in a time of corruption, instability and fear. Take a look around you, and read the headlines. The world is in a panic, as if it is slowly spinning out of control. Not unlike today, Josiah also lived in a time when corruption was rampant in Israel, and the land was in desperate need of revival.

Josiah the Reformer

At the time that Josiah's birth was prophesied, the nation of Israel was in crisis. Yet in the midst of the upheaval, God sent a prophet to prophesy about the future. The man of God prophesied that a young man named Josiah was going to come. (See 1 Kings 13:1–6.)

Note that Josiah's birth was prophesied three hundred twenty-two years before he was born. Do you know what that tells us? God has a destiny and purpose for all of us to fulfill. God knew there was going to be a need for a Josiah in a time of utter chaos and confusion long before he was born. GOD IS NEVER CONFUSED! God is never wondering, "How will we touch the American culture?"

This is the same message I told twenty-five young people a month after I got to Marysville. I preached vision, purpose and the cross. I told them that we were going to carry the cross to this generation. Little did I know that in six years, we would have a youth church of more than eight hundred young people, with visitors coming from twenty states and six nations, as well as attracting media attention.

Prophecy Fulfilled

Between the prophetic word and its fulfillment, there were sixteen different kings before Josiah was born. That tells us that a prophetic word will be fulfilled. Though it may tarry, we are to wait for it. (See Habakkuk 2:3.) Some of you have had words spoken over your life, but you have not seen them come to pass yet. Some of you have wanted to turn your world upside down long before you started reading this book. Do not give up!

In 2 Chronicles 34, Josiah comes on the scene. Josiah was eight years old when he became king. Personally, I do not think it would be that great of an idea to have an eight-year-old as president today. But God IS looking for young people who are anointed and filled with His purpose to go out and turn the world over.

A Josiah Generation for Today's World

The Josiah Generation will be made up of young people and Christians who are totally focused on the vertical—enabling them to impact the horizontal. If you want to impact a culture, you are not going to do it by going after the culture first. *You have to go after God first.*

I have spent seventeen years of my life ministering. At first, I would always preach about witnessing. The problem was, my young people were spiritually dead. They had no fire, passion and unction in them. They were just trying to survive; they were just trying to make it. They were just trying to go through life without backsliding. And here I was saying, "Let's turn our world upside down!"

I soon learned that if you want to take your world, the first thing you have to do is get your young people or church to focus on God. We must get the vertical going.

I do not believe it is a coincidence that Josiah's name means "fire." Have you noticed what many men and women of God have been praying for lately? That is right: fire. I do not think it is a coincidence. People want the fire of God again. Don't you?

Let's look again at 2 Chronicles 34:1–3:

> Josiah was eight years old when he became king, and he reigned in Jerusalem thirty-one years. He did what was right in the eyes of the LORD and walked in the ways of his father David, not turning aside to the right or to the left. In the eighth year of his reign, while he

was still young, he began to seek the God of his father David. In his twelfth year he began to purge Judah and Jerusalem of high places, Asherah poles, carved idols and cast images.

We need to fall in love with Jesus again. Josiah went after God with all his heart, and then he began to affect the horizontal.

Three Stages of Josiah's Reform/Revival

Josiah initiated three stages to revival.

1. Josiah sought God for himself.

You are never too young to become serious about seeking God. Josiah sought God for himself while he was still young. He was only sixteen. That tells me that even sixteen-year-olds today can seek God and know Him.

2. Josiah sought after the God of David.

You need to find heroes in the faith. If you have no heroes and no one to emulate, you need to say, "God, give me somebody." Desire to know the God of Billy Graham, Smith Wigglesworth, Moses and David. Why can't we be like Paul in Ephesus, where he caused a riot of revival? Maybe it is because we do not know God as he did. Seek God because you want to know Him, not because you want something from Him. How is your prayer life? You can never seek God too much. I am talking about impacting your culture. I am talking about seeking the God of your father David. Josiah knew that David was a man after God's own heart, and he wanted to know the God of his father.

Do not rely on your friends, church or pastor to help you seek God—you need to seek God for yourself. Every great leader must seek God wholeheartedly. In the Bible, Jesus, Paul, Moses and everyone who had an impact in the world spent time apart with God.

> Jesus replied: "'Love the Lord your God with all your heart and with all your soul and with all your mind.' This is the first and greatest commandment. And the second is like it: 'Love your neighbor as yourself.' All the Law and the Prophets hang on these two commandments."
>
> —MATTHEW 22:37–40

The Josiah Generation will consist of people who are determined to seek God even if it means pursuing Him alone. The kingdom of God is based upon relationship and knowing somebody—knowing their spirit and heart. If you want to turn your world upside down, you have to go after the one who can do it—Jesus Christ.

3. Josiah rooted out and rebuilt.

You need to root out what is not of God and rebuild your spiritual life. You must root out and rebuild. Josiah knew that there was no use destroying something unless he had something better to replace it with. The Josiah Generation needs not only to destroy and hate sin, but also must want to rebuild the temple—God's kingdom.

The Importance of God's Book

After the Book of the Law was found, Josiah knew how far he and his people had strayed.

> While they were bringing out the money that had been taken into the temple of the LORD, Hilkiah the priest found the Book of the Law of the LORD that had

been given through Moses. Hilkiah said to Shaphan the secretary, "I have found the Book of the Law in the temple of the LORD." He gave it to Shaphan.

Then Shaphan took the book to the king and reported to him: "Your officials are doing everything that has been committed to them. They have paid out the money that was in the temple of the LORD and have entrusted it to the supervisors and workers." Then Shaphan the secretary informed the king, "Hilkiah the priest has given me a book." And Shaphan read from it in the presence of the king. When the king heard the words of the Law, he tore his robes.

—2 CHRONICLES 34:14–19

Just as Josiah turned back to the Law, we in this generation need to get back to the Word of God. If we rediscover the Bible, we will see how far we have strayed. Notice what happened when they got back into the Word of God: A passion for God exploded in a greater way—they cleansed the temple. (See 2 Kings 23:1–7, 21–23.)

- Josiah cleansed the house of all remaining gods. (See 2 Kings 23:10–14.)

- Josiah celebrated the Passover. (See 2 Kings 23:21.)

The Passover is a remembrance of what God did for the Israelites in Egypt and how He supplied their needs.

Five Keys to Josiah's Revival

1. **Josiah knew he had to pray.** As Josiah began to pray for revival, God began to do a work in his life.

2. **Josiah was an activist.** He took action regarding his beliefs.

3. **Josiah was honest about sin.** He was transparent about his own sin and the sin of his people.

4. **Josiah rediscovered the Word of God.** He began reading the Scriptures.

5. **Josiah called others to come with him.** In gathering other laborers, Josiah impacted his generation.

Examine Your Ways

You need to have the mentality that "everything starts with me." The model for a powerful life that impacts the world starts with you. If you want a church that prays—it does not matter if you are a children's, youth, singles' or senior pastor—guess who needs to pray? You must do it. If we want to impact our culture with a ministry that is effective, we must examine our ways.

Like Begets Like

The first principle found in the Word of God is in Genesis 1:20–24—the law of reproduction. Like begets like. God said that you will reproduce after your own kind—both the good and the bad. Therefore, if you have a love for the Scripture, you will inspire people around you who also will love the Word. If you love to worship God, you will inspire others to worship God.

People will follow what you do more than what you say. What you want to see in the culture is who you have to become. We are the first obstacle for Jesus in turning our world upside down. We must become pregnant with vision and passion in order to give birth to a successful ministry.

Reflector of God's Freedom

The Corinthian church was like today's Charismatic and Pentecostal congregations. They were not lacking in power, but they were lacking in other things. The Corinthians needed to become reflectors of God. (See 2 Corinthians 3:17–18; 4:1–6.)

In 2 Corinthians 3:18, we discover the principle of reflecting God's image—not our own.

> And we, who with unveiled faces all reflect the Lord's glory, are being transformed into his likeness with ever-increasing glory, which comes from the Lord, who is the Spirit.

Reflector of God's Glory

All of us reflect the Lord's glory. The Spirit of God indwells us and has given us the Lord's glory to reflect and shine into a dark generation. Josiah had a dark generation that preceded him. But he allowed the glory of God to shine.

What does *glory* mean?

- The word *glory* means to be held in highest esteem. Jesus gave us the glory that the Father gave Him. (See John 17:22–24.)

- The word *glory* in the Greek means "an opinion, an estimate or the honor resulting from a good opinion" and "the character, especially God's righteousness."

God holds us in the highest esteem because His character of righteousness has been given to us. We are being transformed more and more into His likeness. Our character changes more into the image of Christ. This happens when we reflect in our lives the Word and not the world. We go from glory to glory and from strength to strength, which come from the Lord. (See 2 Corinthians 3:18.)

When you get into that positional place where the Son is shining on you—with no distractions, no bitterness, no unforgiveness—people will see the bright reflection of Jesus in you.

Reflectors of God's Example to Us

> Follow my example, as I follow the example of Christ.
> —1 Corinthians 11:1

We reflect God's glory by example. And because we are examples, the Bible says that:

- We must renounce secret and shameful ways.
- We are not to use deception.
- We cannot distort the Word of God.

If we do not renounce our secret shameful ways, God will reveal them publicly. Have you ever heard someone say, "I don't have the heart for it"? You do not have the heart—God has the heart and He put it in you, just as He put it within the prophet Nehemiah who had the "heart" to rebuild the fallen walls of Jerusalem in Nehemiah 4:6–10.

> Let us not become weary in doing good, for at the proper time we will reap a harvest if we do not give up.
> —Galatians 6:9

Keys to Setting an Example

1. **Spend time with people who can be an example to you.** If possible, hang out with people that have been in ministry for more than thirty years. Find a senior saint, and let him or her mentor you.

2. **Be accountable to someone.** The Bible says to confess your sins one to another.

3. **Have a clear conscience.** In 2 Corinthians 4:2, the Bible says we commend ourselves to every man's conscience. Is there anyone you know with whom you do not have a clear conscience? You need to have a clear conscience with everyone.

Reflectors by Servanthood

We need to learn that we reflect the glory of God by servanthood, which changes us quicker than almost anything does. People respond to servanthood. What better way is there to turn a world upside down than by serving it? Josiah served his people, and God blessed him for it.

Reflectors in a Dark Generation

God has made His light shine in our hearts and has given us the knowledge of His glory so that we can go out and give it to those that need it. (See Romans 6:19–22; 2 Corinthians 4:5–6.)

God is eager to manifest His reviving presence and power in every generation. But we must take steps to prepare for the release of His fullness in our midst. On the eve of their passage over Jordan into the Promised Land, Joshua charged the children of Israel to prepare their hearts. "Consecrate yourselves, for tomorrow the Lord will do amazing things among you" (Josh. 3:5). The psalmist understood the importance of spiritual preparation for revival. "Righteousness shall go before him; and shall set us in the way of his steps" (Ps. 85:13, KJV).

Steps of Action

1. **Pray** the prayer of the psalmist: "Search me, O God, and know my heart; try me, and know my anxieties: and see if there is any wicked way in me, and lead me in the way everlasting" (Ps. 139:23–24).

2. **Be totally honest** with God.

3. **Agree with God** about each wrong He reveals in your life. Confess each sin, with the willingness to make it right and forsake it.

4. **Praise God** for His cleansing and forgiveness.

5. **Renew** your mind and **rebuild** your life through meditation and practical application of the Word of God.

A Man Who Turned His World Upside Down

Less than ninety years ago, there was another young man who was not afraid to call his compatriots to confession and repentance. He was Evan Roberts, age twenty-six, of Wales.[1] Roberts, a student at Newcastle Emlyn College, had a profound experience with God in which he experienced cleansing and awakening in his own life. With the permission of his college principal, Roberts left his studies and went home to the village of Loughor to preach his first sermon. Only seventeen people waited to hear his first message, but he gave them four points:

1. Confess any known sin to God, and make right any wrong done to man.

2. Put away any doubtful habit.

3. Obey the Holy Spirit promptly.

4. Confess faith in Christ openly.

No one could have imagined the response. Dr. J. Edwin Orr said that within three months, a hundred thousand converts had been added to the churches of Wales. Five years later, a book debunking the revival was published, and the main point made by the scholarly author was that of the hundred thousand added to the churches, only eighty thousand remained.

Roberts was not afraid to call sin by its name, not in a self-righteous sense. He emphasized cleansing and forgiveness, and then encouraged others to do the same. In doing so, he turned his world upside down.

This book was born through my life experiences with the Lord—both as a Christian and minister. As you have read this final chapter, it is my prayer that you have seen yourself differently—as God sees you. That is the only way that our world has any chance of surviving. We need a generation—your generation—to pick up the slack that my generation has neglected and left behind. We need a powerful generation of young people willing to pay the price to turn their world upside down.

TURNING UPSIDE DOWN

1. Apply the story of Josiah to your own life.

2. Where is your sphere of influence?

3. What things and people can you affect?

4. Can you stand up for righteousness in the things that are happening around you?

5. Are you truly living out a pure life, day in and day out?

6. What is your vision for your life, school and family?

7. Write down a hit list of people you plan to influence and target for salvation. Pray over that list daily.

Notes

Chapter 9
Part 1: Winning the Giant Battle

1. Jon Johnstone, *Christian Excellence* (Grand Rapids, Mich.: Baker Book House, 1995), 94.

Chapter 14
The Reality of Hell

1. Joachim Jeremias, *The Parables of Jesus*, 2nd rev. ed. (New York: Scribners, 1972), 184; as quoted in Dr. Ralph E. Wilson, "#71: The Rich Man and Lazarus (Luke 16:19–31)," retrieved from Internet at JesusWalk, www.jesuswalk.com/16_19-31.htm.

Chapter 16
The Weapon of Worship

1. Jack Hayford, ed., *The Spirit-Filled Life Bible* (Nashville, Tenn.: Thomas Nelson, 1999), s.v. "Kingdom Dynamics."

Chapter 19
A Person of Passion

1. Tom Carter, ed., *2200 Quotations From the Writings of Charles H. Spurgeon* (Grand Rapids, Mich.: Baker Books, 1988), 183.

2. Charles Finney, *The Autobiography of Charles G. Finney* (Minneapolis, Minn.: Bethany House, 1977), 15.

3. Ibid, 22.

4. Carter, *2200 Quotations From the Writings of Charles H. Spurgeon*, 57.

Chapter 23
Upside-Down Destiny

1. The story on Evan Roberts was adapted from an article by Dr J. Edwin Orr, a leading scholar of revivals who published detailed books about evangelical awakenings. His research discovered major spiritual awakenings about every fifty years, following the Great Awakening from the mid-eighteenth century, in which John and Charles Wesley, George Whitefield and Jonathan Edwards featured prominently. This article, based on one of Edwin Orr's messages, is adapted from articles reproduced in the National Fellowship for Revival newsletters in New Zealand and Australia. © Renewal Journal #1 (93:1), Brisbane, Australia, pp. 1318. Used with permission.

To learn more about Benny Perez, his ministries and materials, please contact:

Pacesetters International
P. O. Box C
Marysville, WA 98270
(360) 658-6238
E-mail: info@pacesetters.org
www.pacesetters.org

The Church at South Las Vegas
2505 Anthem Village Drive
Suite E-549
Henderson, NV 89052
(702) 361-1579
E-mail: info@thechurchlv.com
www.thechurchlv.com

Are you ready to change your world?

We pray that God's overflowing power has changed the course of your life through this message. Isn't it exciting to know that you can impact history and make a difference in your family, community, nation and even the world? Here is another book from Charisma House that offers awesome suggestions for your spiritual journey.

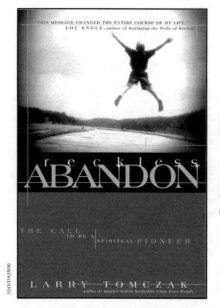

A new day is dawning for Christianity, and this book is your manual for stepping into your call and experiencing a new frontier for the kingdom.

0-88419-876-6
$13.99

Take your faith to the next level!